ANY B
BISCUITS?

David Mcclure

BABU
PUBLISHING

Published in 2021 by Babu Publishing

ISBN Paperback: 978-1-7399866-0-5
Ebook: 978-1-7399866-1-2

Published with the help of Indie Authors World
www.indieauthorsworld.com

IndieAuthors
World

I would like to dedicate this book to my mother, Carol, who dedicated so much of her short life to looking after myself and all of my brothers and sisters so well. Also to my long suffering wife Martha, who has spent the best part of the last fifty years listening to all these stories many times over. Now the stories are in print, perhaps she won't need to hear them any more. Last but not least, to my grandson Lewis who is an avid reader and to my granddaughter Holly who learned to read during lockdown so that she would be able to read this book.

Acknowledgements.

To Indie Authors World without whom this book would not have been possible. Particularly Kim & Sinclair MacLeod who have shown me so much patience. All of my immediate family, new and old, gave me lots of encouragement to continue with writing. Martha, Amanda, David, Billy, Danielle. Also my friends, Stuart, Paul, Bill, Helen, Pat, Robert & Jane.

I cannot thank you all enough.

Chapter 1

Up and into school

"Give me oil in my lamp keep it burning
Give me oil in my lamp I pray"

I am up for my breakfast. Fed, dressed, then out. It's a nice sunny and frosty Spring morning and I am running up the Avenue with my new "Tacketty Boots" on. Along past the clinic to the roundabout. Over the zebra crossing then down to the shops. Oh!!! Mmmmm!!! The different smells of fresh baked bread and rolls coming out of Irvine's the Bakers are amazing. Some nice ladies working here.

"Any broken biscuits?" I ask from the door.

"Sorry Wee Davie, no broken biscuits this morning," says Jenne.

"Oh well, can I come in after school to see if there are any?" I ask.

"No problem, son," says Jenne.

Back out the bakers I go, down past Fairfulls the butchers where two women are outside gossiping about someone else's misfortune. Standing there with pipe cleaners in their hair, head scarfs and wrap-around pinnies on, and the nylons rolled down to the top of their slippers, exposing lazy tartan legs, caused by sitting too close to the fire for long periods. They have a real cheek to talk about anyone else, the state they are in.

On I go, down past the Co op to cross at the lollipop man with his Captains style hat and hi-viz uniform on. The General, we called him, because he was very tall and always saluted everyone who crossed the road and he also saluted the traffic for stopping for him.

Into Gartsherrie Primary school (a huge red sandstone building) which is now dull and dark grey with the dirt gathered over many years of being next to the Iron works.

The playground is starting to fill up, no time to search for my pals, nearly time to go into school. I run round the back of the building where we all line up in our classes waiting for the teacher to come out with the bell. I push myself to the front as I want to run with the bell.

"Here you go David." The head teacher Mr Russell says, handing me the large brass bell. Brilliant, away I go, running round the outside of the school building, ringing the bell as loud as I could ring it. CLANG... CLANG... CLANG, Letting the stragglers know it was time for school. These new Tacketty Boots were doing a grand job carrying me all the way round the playground and back into the school where everyone else is in class now. The bell is placed on the shelf inside the door then I have to hurry into my class where I sit three rows from the front.

Miss Brydon, my teacher who is also the deputy head-mistress, is already handing out reading books. Reading a book is one of my favourite pastimes so English lessons were, in the main, quite enjoyable for me. My pet hate in class was when we all had to take it in turns to stand up and read a paragraph from "The Reading Book." I quickly stopped listening as some of my classmates were struggling to mouth simple words and sentences, so, I just continued reading and became so engrossed, that when it came to my turn I was already four pages ahead and could not read the next paragraph when I was asked. I was in trouble quite often, for, "not paying attention."

We had a milk break in the morning. A crate of milk was brought in and we all filed out to the front of the class to get a straw and a little glass bottle which was a third of a pint of milk, which we took back to our desks to drink.

One morning the milk came in and we were told to come out and get it. I noticed Big Lorraine next to me was sleeping so I gave her a gentle shove and told her the milk was here. Well!! An EXPLOSION happened!! Or so I thought. Miss Brydon came storming down between the desks shouting at me. "Who do you think you are, waking someone up like that?" She grabbed my arm and marched me over to the SANDBOX which is a huge Blue painted wooden chest that held all the toys and crafty stuff for the class. She bent me over the sandbox (6 yrs old at the time, I was still in short trousers) and she gave me five hard slaps on the back of my thighs. This was absolute agony, I had never felt pain like it. I was used to a "cuff on the lug" from mam for misdemeanours, this was a whole other level. Determined not to cry in front of the class I went back to my seat with my lip trembling and had difficulty sitting on the hard wooden seat. My memory of that incident is still strong in my mind, many years later. Nevertheless, I had to sit with my leg sore for the rest of the day and try to look interested in what was going on.

Big Lorraine never ever said a word to me about the incident so I moved my seat a bit further away from her. Seemed to me she was some kind of teacher's pet as I had heard other classmates getting into trouble for nodding off but not big Lorraine.

THE SANDBOX I had been smacked over earlier in the day contained loads of goodies for the crafts we did for the last hour in the afternoon. We sometimes made table mats, tea cosies and coasters to take home. Bean bags, skittles, paints and crayons were all in there too. Although I was wary of the box now, I still loved the contents. The bell rings, it's home time, we are free to go. Miss Brydon is at the classroom door putting on her blue coat with the fox fur collar when she stops me and says,

"I hope you have learned your lesson then Mcclure."

I ask her. "Is that a real dead fox you are wearing?"

"Get out of here you," she says.

Jumping past her like lightning in case a skelp was coming my way, I ran outside. Over the wall to the sanny hole, School is out for the day. Yippee.

Chapter 2

Schools out, Treehouse here I come

"Mr Noah built an Ark the people thought it such a lark"

I sometimes escaped out of the school by going over the back wall to the sanny hole. Down through the trees and through the gap in the iron fence that takes me into my back garden. Five minutes takes me home. The school bag is put into my room under the bed and I change into old clothes to go out and play, then I remember, if I hadn't taken the shortcut through the sanny hole I wouldn't have forgotten to go and see if there were any broken biscuits at the bakers.

I shout to Mam, "Can I get a piece n jam?"

"OK laddie, here you are," she says.

I grab the piece and head down the stairs and back outside to see who is about. Mam shouts, "Remember to be back for your dinner."

"OK, I will," I shout back.

I can hear some hammering up in the tree house which is about forty feet up in a huge oak tree in the woods at the bottom of the avenue. Slipping through the iron gate I run over to the huge tree and start to climb up. The climb used to be quite hard until Tam, my pal, nailed on some pieces of wood for makeshift steps for part of the way up, then, when you reached the lower branches that made it easier to get right up to the place where we had made a platform about six feet by six feet. This was the base for the tree-house which was always a work in progress.

Tam was always working on some project or another and today was no different. He was a year older than me and I always looked to see what he was up to next. Tam had access to his father's tools, hammer, axe, nails and screws. This was great as we could make lots of things we needed for the treehouse.

"Howz it gaun Tam?" I said, when I reached the platform.

"Aye, great Davie. I am just nailing a few bits of widd on the side here to stop the wind and rain from getting in."

"Great stuff," I say. "That will make it a lot better".

"I have found more widd up the sanny hole at the back of the clinic, do you want to help me get it down here?" he asks me.

"OK," I say. "But we need to go now so that I can get back for my dinner."

"Right, let's go." Said Tam.

Off we went, up round the perimeter fence towards the sanny hole. This takes us behind the houses we stay in and round behind the clinic at the top of the street where the pile of widd has been heaved over the fence. Some workmen doing work in the clinic earlier did not have enough room on their barrow to take it away so it was dumped over the fence.

This is great for us as we could use all of these broken planks in the treehouse. Tam and I get a few planks under each oxter and head back to the treehouse. It was a bit of a hard slog but we managed to get all the widd down to the bottom of the big tree in three trips.

"Now we need to get it up the tree," I say.

"No problem there Davie," says Tam.

He dives into a large rhododendron bush and crawls underneath and comes back out with a long thick rope.

"Right Davie, I will go up the tree with the rope and you can stay down here and tie on the widd, then I will haul it up."

So, that is exactly what we did. Within half an hour all the widd was safely stored up in the tree house. We only had one mishap when one of the loads being hauled up came undone half way up the tree as my limited granny knot was not good enough and the whole lot landed back down beside me. "Phew! That was too close Tam." I say.

"Stop messing about Davie and send up the widd," was his reply.

"David, dinner is ready." I could hear mam shout.

"That's me Tam, I need to go now, so, I will see you later."

"Aye me too," says Tam. "I will come down for you later and we can maybe do some more work up here."

"OK, let's go." I said.

We hurry home for our dinner. I stay in an upstairs flat three doors up the tree lined, Colt Avenue, Tam lives eight doors further up the street. I hurry up the stairs, I can smell the dinner and can hear the clacking of cutlery on the plates as my brothers and sisters are already at the table and tucking in.

Mams cooking is great. I squeeze into a space at the table and Mam puts my dinner down in front of me. Oh my!! One of my favourite dinners. Mince and tatties. Dinner is soon finished and the plates are all cleared. We put the empty plates in the sink to be washed.

My older sisters Jinty and Claire usually do the washing up to help our mam as she is often busy with the younger ones. Six of us sat down at the table to be fed. Not a scrap is left on the plates.

Mam has had a busy afternoon cooking in the kitchen as always. If she is not cooking then she is cleaning, washing or ironing but at six or seven years of age I take it all for granted. Everything at home at that age, happens as if by magic.

Tam is now at the door for me.

"Can I go out to play now Mam?" I say.

"Sure son," she says. "Mind and be back before dark."

"OK Mam, I will."

Our Sanny asks, "Can I come too?"

"Right, come on then," I say.

Our Sanny has just turned five, so I will need to look after him while he is with me. Sanny is strong so he will be a good help haudin the widd up in the tree house while Tam and I nail it on.

Back up in the tree house, we only have an hour until dark but Tam says not to worry and he pulls out two candles and a box of matches. Tam never ceases to amaze me how he always has everything he needs to hand. We are sitting by candle light admiring our work not because it is dark outside but because it is dark in the treehouse as we forgot to make a window. That will be a job for another day. Time to get home as it will be really dark soon. A good day today. Cannot wait to get back to the tree house tomorrow.

Sanny and I get back in the house and Mam says,

"Have you boys got any homework to do? If so, get it done now then it will soon be time for bed."

"Homework is all done," I say.

Our Sanny says. "I never get any homework as I am too young."

"OK," says Mam. "You can all have some tea and toast if you go and sit in the living room quietly as your Daddy is getting out of bed for his dinner just now, then he is going out on the night shift."

We all sit in the living room quietly waiting on the toast coming through the hatch in the wall from the scullery. I decided to tell our Claire about the smacking I got this morning over the sandbox. She says, "Keep it to yourself David, or you might cause more trouble."

I never quite worked out why this may be the case but I never mentioned it again to anyone.

We are either writing or drawing at the table. We do not have a television so the radio is on the 'Light Programme' quietly in the background. We hear Daddy in the kitchen getting his dinner. He puts his head round the door after his dinner and says to us,

"Are you all OK then?"

"Yes," we all chorus. "We are just drawing with our colouring pencils before we go to bed."

"OK then, I am off to the night shift now, don't forget, I will blow the PUG Whistle at five minutes to eight in the morning to get you up for school."

"Great, we will all be listening," we tell him.

Daddy drives a PUG which is a small steam engine in Gartsherrie Iron Works. At night, looking out of our scullery window and away beyond the sanny hole, in the distance, we can see the Iron Works furnaces belching out fire, with multi-coloured smoke, sparks and steam which is lighting high up into the night sky and can be seen for miles around. If Mam opens the scullery window in the morning we will hear the PUG whistle blowing to let us know it is nearly time to get up for school.

"It is bedtime now, you lot, so let's go," Mam says.

No hugs and cuddles before bed for us in those days, just a nice pat on the head or a friendly cuff on the back of the lug as we troop past Mam who is standing at the scullery door.

"No nonsense now." We are told.

No argument from us as we troop up the long lobby past all the coats hanging up, then into our rooms. (Under the coats in the lobby is where mam and all the girls hide when there is thunder and lightning outside.) The boys have their own room and the girls have their own room. My bed is the top bunk in the boys room and Our Sanny is at the bottom. My other two younger brothers share a double bed. We all strip off in the dark down to a wee short simmit. No pants or pyjamas for us. We think the new "twin tub washing machine" is eating our pants and socks as there always seems to be a shortage of both. Normally we go to bed in the dark as the light bulb is broken. We have a quick pillow fight. (that is what broke the light bulb) My two youngest brothers Wullie and Shug usually get a friendly pummelling from us two older boys. Before getting into bed our Sanny asks me what to do with the chewing gum he has been chewing. As it still has some flavour he did not want to throw it away. We are not allowed chewing gum but Sanny has got some from one of his pals.

"Put it behind your ear then you can get it again in the morning." I tell him. We settle down quietly into bed, thinking all about today's adventures and look forward to tomorrow.

Very quietly, we all drift away into the land of nod.

Little did I know the trouble there would be in the morning when we got up and Mam discovered our Sanny's chewing gum all sticky and gooey and stuck at the back of his lug and all through the side of his hair. Making my escape down the stairs eating my toast I can hear our Sanny telling mam.

"Our David tellt me to do it, so it is his fault."

Later that day when everything had calmed down and our Sanny, sporting a rather odd lopsided haircut, admitted to me, he knew I was only joking when I said. "Put the gum behind your lug."

He just did it anyway.

Chapter 3

Saturday, time to go to work.

"The wise man built his house upon the rock"

Saturday Arrives.

No school today, no long lie in for me either. Great, I have a really exciting day ahead. I am going down to the Gartsherrie Iron work this morning with Daddy's piece. He usually forgets his piece on a Saturday. This is my pass at the security gate to deliver his piece box to him. Security and health & safety is very slack in those days. The men on the entrance gate know me anyway. "On you go then Davie, you know where to go."

I am ushered through the huge gates and head diagonally across the yard towards a whole load of buildings with a multitude of different iron work processes going on in them. This place is like a small town. It has a lot of different tradesmen working away at their various tasks in different buildings. Blacksmiths, joiners, electricians, engineers, even cobblers and a paint shop and various other maintenance shops. Some of the smells are quite pungent coming from the different workshops. Up between these meandering buildings I go, running across a bouncy plank of wood which is over a channel of hot multi-coloured cooling water, which is flowing away from the furnaces towards the tarryburn.

There, in all its glory, stands "The Bothy."

This is a fairly large brick building with a smoking chimney on top. A magical place for me. Chapping the door of the bothy I stand back as the door is opened by a huge old man with a purple face and he says to me,

"Oh! It's you wee Davie, come on on on on in, you don't need to knock." Auld Wullie welcomes everyone with this strange phrase, (come on on on on in).

Auld Wullie had been retired ten years before at the age of seventy, when the company decided he should. On Friday of that week at a retirement ceremony in the office, he was presented with a large mantel clock from the Company, accompanied by some other gifts from all his workmates then on to a party at the pub to celebrate. The following Monday at six a.m Auld Wullie was back at his post as usual, in the bothy. The Gaffer came in and reminded him that he was retired. Auld Wullie was having none of it.

"I need to come to work, I have nobody at home. The people here have been my family for forty years so I will carry on if you don't mind, and, if you need the gifts back I will bring them in tomorrow."

After some discussion between the Management and the Gaffer, it was decided to let Auld Wullie carry on working and no need to bring back the gifts. Auld Wullie continued happily working for many more years until the Iron Work was closed in 1967.

The Bothy is a place that takes your breath away. With the heat from a huge urn full of boiling water on a gas ring in one corner and a great roaring coal fire in the other. A long table down the middle of the room with bench seating down each side is where the men will sit when they come in to have their pieces. Auld Wullie is "THE NIPPER" which is the title of the guy whose job it is to keep the fire going and the urn full of constantly boiling water for the tea, as the workmen come in for their tea at different times during the day. He is busy putting the tea cans out because he knows who is due in, so I help him with this. Then, I go out and fill the coal scuttle for the fire. Auld Wullie toasts some pieces on cheese on a long fork at the fire for some of the men as he knows when they will be in for a break.

The tea is made in tin cans which have a wire handle. All the men have dry tea and sugar which is kept in a small brass coloured box which is an oval shaped cylinder with a lid at each end. The piece box always amazes me as it is the shape of a slice of plain bread. When the pieces have been made up, (8 slices) they are placed in the two sided box which slides together to keep them fresh.

The men who are chattering loudly start to come in for their piece and I try to stay out of the way. "Howz it Gaun wee Davie? Are you here with your oul man's piece?" They say.

"Aye, I am." I say.

What I really want to say is, do not call Daddy the "Oul Man" as he won't like it. Just then "the oul man" comes in, to a whole load of cat calls and banter from the men about him using me as a slave to bring his piece to work for him.

The atmosphere in the Bothy is very cheery and the men are full of chat and banter about their previous nights drinking in the pub. (A lot of men in those days spent a lot of money and time in the pub.) Maybe that is why Coatbridge Main Street had a pub on every corner then.

I learned a few strange new words that day, which I know I need to keep to myself. One or two of the "Oul man's" friends dig deep in their pockets to give me a few coins to spend as payment for me helping Auld Wullie in the bothy. "Grossin Tam" the shunter comes in and says to me, "Hello wee Davie, long time no see."

Then he pats me on the head and ruffles my hair then claps me on the back and rubs me hard on both cheeks with his huge hands. Little did I know that his hands were covered in soot and now so was my face. All the men in the bothy were laughing and said to him,

"Aye Grossin Tam, you are some man so you are."

Not realising I was the bothy entertainment I settled myself down on the end of the bench to have my own piece, which Mam made up for me. Drinking hot tea from the can is awkward and I manage to burn my mouth more than once. Not to worry, the best of the day is yet to come.

Grossin Tam proceeds to tell everyone in the bothy a story that supposedly happened the week before, about the Co-operative milkman coming out of the stables on Jackson Street with his horse drawn milk float at six a.m in the morning when the horse slipped on the frosty road and landed on its backside. The milkman could not get the horse to move no matter what he tried. Not giving up, the milkman went across the road and asked the lady in one of the houses for a hot tattie.

"These tatties are just on the boil so there you go," she says.

Handing him a hot tattie. He took it from her and juggling it from hand to hand so as not to burn himself he crossed back over the road and lifted the horse's tail and put the roasting hot tattie under it.

"Well!!" says Grossin Tam. "The horse, with its rear end all skint, got up on it's hooves and took off, skidding and sliding so fast that it ripped the front wheels off the milk float and thundered down the hill like Judas's chariot."

Everyone was rolling about laughing at that story. I often wondered after that, why anyone would be boiling tatties at six a.m in the morning.

Enough of Grossin Tam's jokes. Piece time is over and the men start to leave the Bothy to go back to their individual jobs.

"The Oul' man" takes me out and along the track to the "PUG" (No.19) which is standing waiting where he left it just outside the engine shed. The pug has been filled with water and coal for the next part of the shift. "The Oul' man" climbs onto the footplate and turns around to give me a hand up beside him. The heat on the footplate is amazing. The fire door is partly closed but I can still see the white hot flames as the reversing lever is released and we set off with a small pull of the throttle lever. The engine seems to be spitting steam from all sides. "PHweet PHweet PHweet" goes the oul man on the steam whistle, to let the furnace men know we are on our way to pick up the full slag ladles.

Our job today will be to push the full ladles up the slag hill to empty them. Slag is molten rock, which is a bi-product of the furnace's melting process to extract the iron from the ore to make what they call pig iron.

The slag is poured off into the ladles for transportation to the slag hill which is a dumping area two miles away from the main works. I am watching everything that is going on as I know that I will be driving the PUG today. "The oul man" usually drives the pug but he needs a shunter. The shunter is Grossin Tam, whose job it is, with a long wooden pole with a curly hook on it like a pig's tail, is to hook and unhook the wagons and ladles from the PUG. He is going home early today (probably to the pub) so the oul man will be the shunter and I will be the driver of

22

the PUG. We have a little practice run to show me the speed to do. Then, standing on a wooden box on the footplate to operate the huge reversing lever which is on a ratchet going forwards and backwards. After some shunting to and fro, backwards and forwards, moving coal wagons and flat bed wagons here and there about the works the bogies with the full ladles of slag are now cleeked on at the front and we are pushing them up the line through the works and towards the slag hill. The oul man has to climb on and off the pug many times to change the points as we negotiate our way slowly towards the line that takes us up to the slag hill. We have a long flatbed wagon between us and the two ladles which is used as a safety barrier to keep a little distance between us and the searing heat of the molten slag.

"CHUFF CHUFF CHUFF CHUFF." The throttle is open wide and we are pushing hard uphill now and the powerful little pug is really beginning to labour under the strain of the load.

The sight of Steam belching out from the pistons and black smoke pouring from the lum is a sight to behold, as we shovel more coal on the fire.

Across the bridge over the Gartgill burn we travel, then, a long curve up under the Glenboig road bridge. As we go under the bridge all the smoke from the pugs lum is pushed into the cab where we are temporarily blinded until we get out the other side. Our faces are made even more black by the sooty smoke. We do not care, onwards and upwards, climbing all the way to the top of the slag hill, where I know there is a spectacular show yet to come.

Near the top of the hill we level out a bit just before the summit. There is a siding where we have to leave one of the ladles as we can only empty one ladle at a time. The oul man puts the brakes on the ladle we are leaving for now. I reverse out of the siding with one ladle on until the points are changed, then we can head up to the top of the hill to tip the slag. The ladle is simply a huge half round shaped bowl sitting on a set of bogie wheels. When we reach the top I stop the pug and the oul man jumps out to firstly put the brakes on the ladle wheels then unhooks it from the pug. A chain is attached from the ladle to the pug then we reverse to pull the chain which tips the ladle. As the ladle tips, out rolls a huge twenty ton ball of encrusted slag bouncing down over the hill until it hits a piece of old hardened slag which bursts it into a huge flaming explosion of sparks and fire.

Brilliant, I can't wait to go and get the other ladle. The second ladle of slag has cooled a bit more but the result is the same, another twenty ton ball of fire explodes and smashes into thousands of fiery pieces before it reaches the bottom.

The huge mountains of slag waste created over many years by hundreds of Iron Works up and down the Country were discovered by road builders to be good quality bottoming for roads prior to applying Tar Macadam. Until, unfortunately, a cheaper method was found and some of the slag heaps still exist to this day.

We are ready for home now. Trundling back down the hill at speed with our empty wagon and ladles which need to be left near the furnaces for the next shift, we have time to look around us and admire the view as we go past the "Cement Plant," and through the "Coke Plant," past the large Tarry Burn Pond which is a small lake full of all sorts of pollution. We travel along nearly level with the Gartgill Burn which is where we go sometimes to catch "Baggy minnens" (minnows.) We have now dropped off the ladles at the furnaces and pull slowly into the Engine shed to damp down the fire in the pug as it is a few hours until the night shift begins. "The Oul man" tells me he is going to meet Grossin Tam in the pub so I have to go home on my own. This has been a brilliant day but I am dog tired and absolutely covered in soot, grime and coal dust.

Nobody batted an eyelid as I walked home up past the long row. One of the windows in the long row has a large goldfish bowl with a huge goldfish in it. I always stop to look at the fish as I am amazed that such a large fish can survive in this bowl. Maybe the magnifying effect of the bowl has something to do with the size of the fish.

Past Gartsherrie Primary school, looking like a miniature worker and happily jingling the coins I had in my pocket. There were no washing facilities in those days to wash before you went home from work, so, up the road home, as black as I could be.

Passing Irvine the bakers I go in to see if Jenne has "Any broken biscuits" for me. With a big smile she turns round and handing me a large brown paper bag she says, "It looks like you have been working hard today Davie, enjoy your biscuits and tell your mam I was asking for her."

I thanked Jenne very much and wondered how she knew I had been working, as I had forgotten about the colour I was after my day at work on the Pug.

Home at last with the bag of goodies. Mam and my brothers and sisters can't wait to see what is in the bag. Jenne has excelled herself and put a large variety of whole biscuits in with the broken ones. Chocolate ones, Jammie ones, Digestives and Wafer biscuits too, what a feast we had that night after our dinner, which was stovies, corned beef and beetroot, another of our favourites.

Saturday night is bath night where my brother Sanny and I share a bath. I had already scrubbed a lot of the soot off when I came home earlier so the bath water did not get too mucky when I went in. We Baptise each other in the bath which is testimony to a previous church experience we had. After our bath we have to get the bone comb through our hair to get rid of any nits or head lice we may have picked up at school. Heids all suitably bone combed and nipping, then dabbed with suleo (a horrible smelling yellow potion used to kill off anything missed by the bone comb.) We all line up to get a tablespoonful of cod liver oil which is good for you, apparently.

Sanny and I are playing in the living room marching up and down thumping on two National dried milk tins, using them as a drum. The noise must have been awful. Exasperated, mam grabbed the tin off me and clunked me on the head with it. Blood poured down my face so mam rushed me into the kitchen sink and rinsed my hair under the tap and parted it to see what the damage was. No serious damage so my hair was dried and the bleeding stopped really quickly. Mam said she was really sorry and I said I was not bothered as it all happened so quickly and dealt with before I had time to think about it.

It is time for bed again. I am so tired that I do not want to have a pillow fight tonight. Off again drifting into the land of nod.

Chapter 4

Sunday best and up for church

"Onward Christian Soldiers marching as to war"

Rise and shine, Sunday morning, I get up with my brothers and sisters (not too early). We have breakfast of scrambled eggs and toast made by my two big sisters, Jinty and Claire, (to give Mam a long lie.) Then we all get washed and dressed up in our Sunday best. We have Church this morning at eleven o'clock over in Corsewall Street at the Baptist Church. Trooping over the Blair Road we go. It is a twenty minute walk to the church. We all file in as a family. My oldest sister Claire first, then the rest of us in a line following behind. We sit together in the same hard wooden pew, sliding along so that we can all get in. Standing up when the organ music starts, we all join in singing the psalms and hymns, praising the Lord. Everyone all around us seems to be singing at the top of their voice so we think we can belt it out too, which we do with gusto. Mr Service the minister has a good voice that we can listen to, so, during his sermon there is always good behaviour among my brothers and sisters when he is up in his pulpit waving his arms about and laying off at great length about bringing down fire and brimstone upon us. Fire and brimstone reminds me of the slag hill the day before and I can really understand not wanting to bring any of that down upon us. Next, we leave the church with a reminder from the minister for us all to be at the Baptist Sunday School in the afternoon.

Along Water Street we troop, past a part of the old canal which stinks to high heaven, (wee granny's words,) a shortcut through the Central station then past the fountain and half way up Sunnyside road, we arrive at the Salvation Army Citadel which has Sunday School at twelve thirty for an hour. We do not tell anyone in the Baptist church or Sunday school we go here as we think, rightly or wrongly, they might not like it. We go into the hall and are welcomed at the door with big smiles from the nice uniformed ladies who show us where to go.

We are all agog at the Band of Hope as they start to play their different brass instruments and tambourines while marching round the hall in their very smart uniforms. We are also allowed to march round the hall behind the big drum at times, while singing and belting out "Onward Christian Soldiers marching as to war." We think we could all play a tambourine but cannot afford one and the boys and girls who have them would not give us a shot. In my pocket I have a "jews harp" but I do not take it out to join in the music in case anyone laughs.

We trek home thirsty and hungry for lunch.

Mam reminds us all after lunch when it is time to go out again to the Baptist Sunday school. All the way along Lomond Road to Wilton Street bus terminus, then up past St Bartholomew's church and into the Baptist Sunday school for three o clock. This is a very different kind of Sunday school from the Salvation one. We are welcomed in by Mrs Forrester, a really nice lady who is the Superintendent in charge. After a short prayer Mrs Forrester sits at the upright piano and plays while we sing all the Sunday school choruses we know.

"Joy joy my heart is full of joy."

"Deep and wide, deep and wide,
There's a fountain flowing
Deep and wide."

"The wise man built his house upon the rock, house upon the rock
and the rains a came a tumballing down"

"Dropping dropping, dropping dropping, hear the pennies fall,
every one for Jesus, he shall have them all."

This last one, is the song that is sung as the collection box shaped like a wee red church is passed up and down the rows for us to insert our pennies. We are quite poor so we do not all have pennies to put in the box so some of us pretend we put one in and just shake the box. During the afternoon we are separated into different age group classes and as we did not all have a bible in the family I was given one by the young teacher I had, as long as I promised her I would bring it with me every week. This I did faithfully as I did not want to disappoint her.

Year end is here so we are at the Sunday School Prize giving. We all have perfect attendance this year and cannot wait to go up and get our prizes. Claire and Jinty go up to get their prize of a large bible each. Senga and I also go up to get our prize when they call our names. Senga gets a bible too and as I had been told to keep the bible I borrowed, my teacher had given me a choice of books, so I got a Biggles book. Not to be outdone, Sanny, who had a bible of his own given to him by wee granny in Langloan, proudly walked to the front to get his prize. If you had a bible as I said previously, you could get a book of your choice. Sanny had chosen "the OOR WULLIE book." Sanny marched proudly back to his seat and could not wait to get home with his book. We were all keen to get home and read it too. Inside the fly leaf was a gold edged label with Sanny's name on it, "Awarded for Perfect Attendance."

Sometimes after Baptist Sunday school we would be told to go and visit Wee Granny, Auntie Mamie and cousin George in Langloan. This was another three or four miles more to walk. All in all we were happy to do this as long as the weather was good. All day on a Sunday we had to keep ourselves clean and tidy and look presentable at all times, especially going to Wee Grannys, who would inspect us as we all trooped into her house.

Granny would lay off some quotable biblical quotes then quiz us on our teachings of the day and we would have to stand in the middle of the living room floor and sing any new choruses or hymns we had learned. After a nice cup of "tea and a piece" it was time we went home, as Granny would be getting ready to go to the evening Church Service. Granny made sure we were well "happed up" for the long walk home. Off we went, up the Blair Road again, over the canal bridge, past the daisy park then over to the Gartsherrie roundabout, past the clinic, all the while, jingling the few pennies Wee Granny gave us on the way out. Mam would be waiting to collect the pennies as we came up the stairs into the house. There were never any protests as we all knew she needed the cash.

One time during a visit to Granny's house after Sunday school it was decided that my Brother Sanny and I would go to a Baptismal service at the church as we had never seen one. The rest of the family would go home and we would continue on to the church. I remember our Sanny looking at me then saying, "Och no!! Do we need to go?"

Wee Granny was rummaging in the wardrobe for something for us to wear.

"I noticed you are not wearing any ties so I have found a couple of your Uncle Johnnie's neckties for you, it is much nicer if you are properly dressed going to church."

Sanny looked at the ties she was holding up, then looked at me in horror, then back to the garish multi-coloured silk monstrosities that we would have to wear. Wow, we were both shocked to the core. (The ties were actually from Thailand, apparently.) Anyway, Granny proceeded to put the ties on us as we did not know how to tie one. The ties were on us and knotted very nicely.

"Oh dear." Granny says, as she notices the length of them.

Even when she tucked them into our short trousers the ties were hanging out the bottom. Absolutely hilarious. Sanny and I were in stitches and struggling hard not to laugh out loud. We could not look at each other. Not to be beaten, out came Granny with a huge pair of scissors and promptly cut the bottom of both ties shorter and into a "V" shape. Only problem was, the point of the "V" was the wrong way up.

"Oh my." Says Wee Granny laughing.

"Never mind, there is still enough of the tie to tuck into your breeks. Off you go boys and enjoy the service."

Sanny was still looking at me aghast. There was nothing I could do but smile and thank Wee Granny for the ties and the wee threepenny bit she gave us both to put in the collection. We were so glad it was dark outside and nobody could see us, although we still had to go into the light of the church.

We slipped quietly upstairs to the balcony where nobody knew us and this gave us a great view of the proceedings.

What an eye opener. The Baptist service was a whole new level. The participants had to be eighteen to commit their life to God. Up the stairs to the pulpit came the five candidates all looking terrified, like lambs to the slaughter. They had cloaks on and were pretty much naked underneath.

Mr Service was dressed in his usual ministerial regalia but he had large rubber waders on and he stepped down into the floor of the pulpit which was opened up to reveal it was full of water. The candidates now committing their life to the church went down into the pulpit while we, the congregation, sang, or belted out, the Baptismal hymn, "I surrender all." Sanny and I were delighted to learn this new hymn which went on for a long time as the six candidates were one at a time totally immersed by the minister in the pulpit water, they were spluttering as they climbed up out of the pulpit and got handed a towel. Sanny and I were already planning what we would do with this new found information on bath night. We could not wait to get home and tell the rest of the family all about this service.

On the way home we accidentally managed to lose the garish ties over the canal bridge at King Street.

Chapter 5

Time for sledging

"Joy joy my heart is full of joy"

Deep joy indeed, snow has fallen overnight and is lying two or three inches thick. We are all up at the window scraping the ice away from the inside, looking out to see the thick snow.

We do not have a car and there are only two cars in the Avenue so we are not much concerned about travel. If any of the cars need a push up the street, all the kids get behind them and are amazed at the spinning wheels turning the snow into ice as we all put our weight into getting it up the hill. As the car gathers momentum and speeds away from us, we all fall and are left laughing and rolling about in the snow.

Yippee, we all get sent home from school early today because the heating pipes have frozen and the toilets are frozen too.

I do my usual and climb over the wall and run through the sanny hole to go home. The long grass makes the snow even deeper and by the time I get home I am looking like a snowman.

On my way past Tam's back garden I see he is already constructing a very tall snowman. A snowman made out of two big round snowballs is no good for Tam, he is building a tall one made with four medium snowballs standing on top of each other, which makes it nearly six feet tall. The snowballs are fixed together using a wooden stake in between each ball. You cannot see the stakes as they are covered up each time a ball is placed on top.

"Come on Davie?" Tam says, "I need help to put the top one on as it is quite high to get it up."

After the top ball is in place Tam begins flicking water on to the snowman where it will freeze quickly in the frost. When the whole snowman is frozen solid Tam plans to carve out feet, legs, body, arms and head. He shows me the machete he has acquired for carving "the ice man" as he will be called. This will be a cracker of a snowman and Tam will probably dress it up too.

We will come back to this later, as for now, I ask him to go and get his sledge out and I will go and get mine, then we can polish up the runners and begin sledging up and down the Avenue.

The Avenue has fifteen or so houses down each side with spaces in between so there is quite a long sloping run down to the bottom. We are using the pavement as the snowy ice on there is much smoother than the roadway ice for sledging on.

The first run down is quite slow as the snow is not hard packed yet. After we have been down the run a few times it gets faster and faster. Superb, we are having so much fun that we have no concern for the safety of ourselves or others. Some of the other boys and girls come out to play in the snow too, with some strange looking sledges that are obviously home made or made at their dad's work.

A couple of old neighbours come out and throw ashes on the slide in front of their gates to slow us down. This is futile as there are so many of us going so fast that we do not even notice the dummy bit as we charge over the top of it. We make a huge snake of sledges going down the hill with about twenty of us onboard. When we get to the bottom we separate as there are no brakes and we are glad to be able to crash into the huge pile of snow that has gathered there.

When we are sledging we take a run and lie on the sledge on our stomach and use our legs as a rudder and our toes as a brake. Our tackety boots toes take a hammering with this method.

Tam and I are back at the iceman round his back door. He is frozen solid like a tall soldier. Tam has been working on him for an hour or so after his dinner today. He wields the machete expertly, chipping away excess pieces of ice, shaping arms, legs, neck and head. The face is a little grotesque like "Frankenstein's monster." Nevertheless, we are happy with it. I have cleared away all the ice from his feet and our iceman is standing proud and ready to be dressed.

Tam has found some old clothes to dress the iceman with. A bunnet and scarf is placed on his head and neck, a frozen carrot cut neatly for his nose and pieces of coal for the mouth and silver paper rolled up for eyes. (the silvery eyes will shine in the dark.) An army belt around his waist, brush and shovel, one in each arm is placed strategically. This iceman looks ready for work or soldiering.

We have a large pile of ice and snow, so we set too, building an igloo. The igloo is not very big but can accommodate two of us in there comfortably, sitting down. We used some branches of hedging bent over and some of the old clothes left over from the iceman to form a rough igloo shape. The ice pile and some snow combined, helped us to form a half decent igloo. We did not stay in it long as it was really cold in there. Not at all what we expected. Stories at school tell us eskimos are warm and comfortable in their igloos, no way, we thought.

Chapter 6

Going for taddies and baggy minnens.

"Deep and wide, deep and wide,
There's a fountain flowing deep and wide."

Warmer weather has arrived. There will be tadpoles or taddies as we call them in the ponds and small streams down the widds. (woods) Baggy minnens or Minnows will be about also. Our Sanny and Senga are coming with me to see what we can catch up the Gartgill burn. We have quite a walk to get there through the widds, past the ruins of Colonel Colt's overgrown ruined mansion house which still has some of the walls standing to about six feet high. There is a path through the house which is mainly covered in grass and some bramble bushes. Huge buddleia adorn the walls. There is not enough of the house left to be an eerie place but we can still use it as a fort when we play at commandos.

Through the Colonel's house and further along the path we see loads of chestnut trees that we will climb later in the year for "chessies" to make conkers with. Conkers is a great game where you have a large chestnut on the end of a six inch piece of string or a boot lace. Your opponent swings his conker at yours with the intention of smashing it to pieces. If he misses then you get a turn to do the same to his conker.

The oul man saw Sanny and I playing conkers one day and asked for a shot. "OK," we said, "let's go."

Sanny handed him his conker and I got to have first go. Swinging my conker to and fro, I took as hard a swing as I could at the oul man's conker and smashed him really hard, on the knuckle. Well!! His face was a picture as he glowered at me to see if I had done it deliberately. Turning away from us to go back into the house with his throbbing knuckle, he said,

"That's it."

"Ohh, Haa, Haa, Haa."

Our Sanny and I were rolling about the ground holding our sides with laughter. Looking up at the house to see if the oul man was looking out the window we really could not help bursting out laughing again.

Down the path we come to the Tarry burn. This is the large and dangerous pond that we are warned regularly to stay away from. No one knows the depths or the contents of the eerie looking multi-coloured oily water in it. (mainly run off from Gartsherrie iron works) So we stay away from it and skirt round the side.

We get to a large gate that, climbing over it, takes us onto the Gartgill road. Under the Mainline railway bridge we walk and when we turn the corner at the other side we can see the Gartgill burn.

This burn snakes it's way from Glenboig village which used to have a massive brick works and goes round the bottom of the slag hill and flows on through the Gartsherrie iron work to where? We do not know.

Senga has plastic sandals on so she only needs to take off her socks to start wading the burn. Sanny and I start wading in the burn in our bare feet and we can see minnows darting away in front of us. I get out the burn and go up the path a bit and get back in again. With the net we made out of wire coat hangers and an old pair of nylons I told Senga and Sanny to come quickly up the burn chasing the minnows into the net. A good method we thought of but pretty unsuccessful most of the time until we reverse the method to chasing the little fishes down the burn. We catch loads of sticklebacks and minnows along with a whole host of creepy crawlies. The burn is pretty wide here. An hour later we had selected a few minnows for the milk bottle we brought with us. We put some green looking weedy stuff in the bottle for food for them and we are happy with the results. Thoroughly soaked with dashing up and down the burn, Sanny and Senga sit in a nice sunny spot to dry off before heading home.

I have some cuts on my feet from the rocks in the burn but nothing serious. I put my socks and shoes back on and tell Sanny and Senga it is time to go. Unfortunately the minnows only lasted a few days and Mam says not to bring any more home. Any time after that when we went back to the burn to catch minnows we put them back in the water before going home.

This turned out to be of good standing in later life when I took up trout fishing.

At a loose end one day I decided to climb out of the bathroom window onto the cill where I could reach the toilet waste pipe. Using the pipe I could get up onto the roof of the house which is flat and covered with bitumen. What a great view from up here. I sit and survey my surroundings and find a few tennis balls which I throw down to the back garden. Climbing back down the pipe is much harder than going up. Not realising the danger, I climb up and down here often to get to my quiet place. Another problem with me going up on the roof meant the bitumen was getting hairline cracks in it with me walking on it and causing leaks when it rained. Brown circles would appear in the ceilings inside the house sometimes after it rained. My exploits on the roof were kept to myself.

Chapter 7

The Queen Mary

Will your Anchor hold in the storms of life

On our way home from the minnow hunt up the burn with my sister and brother last week, I spotted a huge tree floating out on the Tarryburn. The Queen Mary was back. This is great news as it has not been seen for a long time. The Queen Mary is a huge dead tree that no longer has any bark and is smooth and shiny, also very slippery when wet. The Queen Mary has a hump at the front like a Jumbo jet then sloping down towards the back almost to the water then back up slightly to the rear which was the remnants of a thick branch sticking up at an angle. Looking at it floating in the water about twenty feet long it resembled a shark or a whale to us. My pal Tam and I had been sailing on the Queen Mary the summer before and I knew he would want to repeat the experience, so I could not wait to tell him.

Two days later Tam and I were at a sandy edge of the Tarryburn where the Queen Mary had come to rest after a windy day the day before. Tam had a length of rope with him which he fixed to a large rusty nail sticking out the top of the hump. Using the rope so that we could stop it from drifting away we were ready at last to set sail once more on the back of the Queen Mary. Tam Jumped onto the tail and told me to jump on the front. Seated comfortably sitting astride the Queen's hump, my feet barely dangling in the water and Tam's legs fully in the water at the rear. I pushed off with my makeshift paddle and we moved slowly out to the middle. The Queen has an imperceptible curve to the left which gives us some steering problems. Paddling hard on the left side we steered some kind of path away over to the other side of the water. This took about half an hour. The old Queen is heavily waterlogged now and really makes us struggle to keep her moving. We beach the Queen on the shore at the other side and holding the rope we get off to stretch our legs.

Looking back across the water we can see the back of the island which is an area we had not seen before. The island looks like a cartoon desert island with a tree on top. It is rumoured to be infested with rats so we do not want to go near it.

We pull the Queen Mary along the shore a little and turn her round to try and position her in a way to let us get back to the other side without hitting the back of the island. Pushing off again we head back. On the way, Tam, without any warning and to my horror, fully clothed, jumped off the Queen into the purply green water. His head pops back up and he looks blue. He did not expect it to be so cold. Tam climbs back aboard and I try to hide my laugh. We need to paddle as hard as we can to get Tam back to shore and get dried. Luckily we got back without too much hassle.

Tam strips off to his underpants and spreads his clothes over a bush. Luckily it is quite a nice warm sunny day. While I tie The Queen up for now, Tam runs down as if to push me in the water but I see him out of the corner of my eye and dodge to the side letting his momentum carry him back into the water. Spluttering this time with a mouth full of stinky water he says

"OK, enough is enough Davie, let's get up the road."

Tam is getting dressed when a couple of older boys from Lomond Road appear and asked us,

"How is the water then?"

Tam says, "Aye it was good, not too cold."

Am thinking, that is a lie then, but a good one Tam. They ask if they can have the Queen Mary.

"Help yourself," we say. "We're finished with it."

Tam and I watched them sail away with the rough paddles we had given them and they struggled with the steering at first but soon got the hang of it. Half way across, the guy at the front was standing up holding onto the rope and rocking the Queen trying to make the other guy fall off. After a few attempts at this he fell into the freezing water himself, so he swam to the back end and managed to pull the other guy in beside him. Fully clothed, the guys splashed about a bit then the cold water began to bite. They were trying to climb back onto the Queen when it rolled over revealing the underside which was black, slimy, rotten and covered in leeches. Nevertheless they persevered and got back on only to realise they had lost the paddles. Using their hands they tried unsuccessfully to paddle back to shore. A stiff breeze had got up and was pushing them to the other side. We could do nothing for laughing watching their antics. The guys finally reached the other side safely and Tam was dry and dressed now so we left them to their fate and headed home.

Up the road past Colonel Colts old mansion we run, past the treehouse and through the gate into the avenue. We are both starving after the adventures of the day, so, into our respective houses for something to eat having made arrangements to meet the next day.

Mam has a look at me and says. "Where have you been the day laddie?"

"Just out playing down the widds with Tam," I say.

"No chance son, you have been down at the tarryburn. I can tell, because you are not clean and you are not dirty either, so tell me where you were?"

I tell Mam the whole story about Tam and the boys from Lomond Road falling off the Queen Mary and she ends up laughing and tells me not to go back there as it is a dangerous place. I assured her I will not go back and she seemed happy with that.

"There you go David, have a piece."

She handed me a plate with a sandwich made from a thick heel of plain bread with potted meat on it. *Oh!! brilliant*, I am thinking, as I head back outside where I meet our Sanny coming up the path.

"Where did you get that?" he says.

"It doesn't matter where I got it, there is none left."

I laugh as he scrambles up the stairs to get what I have. Two minutes later he joins me sitting on the front step with his own piece with potted meat on it.

During this time on the step, we try and think about what we are going to get up to next. Sanny says, "Do you remember last year, we were sitting here and we heard Tam up the sanny hole."

"Yes." I said, as I remembered telling Sanny to "Sshh and listen." We could hear in the distance someone chopping wood. It could only be one person, Tam.

We had slipped through the gap in the back fence and up to the sanny hole. Sure enough there was Tam chopping away at a large tree. Tam stops and offers us the axe.

"You guys can take a turn and let me have a break," he says.

"OK," says our Sanny and gets wired into the chopping.

"What's happening then Tam?" I say.

"Bonfire night in three weeks Davie, did you forget?"

"Yip, I did forget Tam, I can go and get the axe we have in the coal house and we can do more chopping before it gets dark."

Running back through the long grass I go through the gap in the fence, upstairs into the house and into the coal bunker and yes, the axe is still there.

Back up in the sanny hole we are beavering away, Tam has the tree down and is making good progress stripping thick branches from it and our Sanny is piling them up neatly. Soon we have a huge pile of logs which we leave in the long grass in the sanny hole. It is getting dark now so we head home knowing the pile of logs will be safe until our return.

Three weeks later, after chopping and stripping another three large trees, we had built a massive bonfire in the clearing behind the houses. Tam had asked me at school that day if I would meet him up at the roundabout after my dinner.

I made my way there and found Tam with the guy he had made with what looked like a huge brown bear sitting with its head slumped down on his bogie. He had dressed it with working mens clothes obviously too big for it. Complete with a woolly scarf and a bunnet, the guy looked great even though it was dark and I could not see it clearly, I was impressed

"Penny for the guy," we shouted when People were passing by.

"Penny for the guy."

"Remember remember the fifth of November."

Some of the people we attracted were also impressed and threw some coins in the empty Ostermilk tin, but not all were impressed enough to give us a penny for the guy. Some adults walked past, shouting all sorts of abuse and calling us beggars, tramps and tinkies. One person who was called John Lumley also shouted abuse at us because he was always getting verbally abused.

While he was working with his little bin barrow sweeping the streets, people called him Joke the Lum.

Well!! Our guy had had enough of this dog's abuse. He leaped up out of the bogie and to the peoples horror, chased them down the street and shouted all sorts of unprintable abuse right back at them. I could not move when I witnessed this. Tam and I were laughing so hard our sides were sore. We were lying across the bogie in stitches when the guy came back. Turns out, Tam's wee brother Boabie wanted to be the guy. I had no idea, it was absolutely brilliant.

We had made a few shillings for a couple of rockets and Penny bangers or Squibs as my Mam used to call them.

Beer bottles and ginger bottles had been collected and returned to their appropriate owners to collect the deposits due on them. This activity gets us another few bob for bangers.

The younger children in the street had been going round the houses collecting old newspapers and magazines for a couple of weeks which they put in the hollow gap we left in the middle of the bonfire.

One of the trees we had chopped down was so large that we had to roll it down towards the bonfire. We found the huge log was too heavy for us to stand up with the other logs on the bonfire so we just left it far enough away from the bonfire and used it as a bench for us all to sit on.

Bonfire night is here and we are all at the "Bonny" which has not been lit yet. We wait till six oclock when all the boys and girls of all ages from the street have gathered for the spectacle. Some mums and dads are there as well to look out for the younger children to keep them safe.

Tam climbs to the top of the bonfire to place the guy. Brother Boabie has now been replaced as the guy by a huge monkey that Tam had found somewhere, (probably the coup.) Suitably positioned securely on top with his jacket pockets stuffed with newspapers and a few bangers for a surprise effect and smiling down on the rest of us, the guy is sitting proudly.

The time has come and at the end of three weeks of hard work, the honour goes to Tam to light the bonfire. The bonfire is about ten feet tall with the guy on top, so with a length of wood wrapped in a paraffin rag at the end, which Tam lights. Off he goes running round the bottom of the bonfire lighting up all the rolled up papers we have left sticking out. A huge cheer goes up from everyone as, with a "roar and a whoosh," the whole bonfire lights up all at once. As the large pile of old papers and rags inside the bonnie soaked in paraffin catches fire, we can hear loud crackling as the widd on the inside takes hold. Smoke is billowing up and around the monkey guys' lugs now. A real spectacle to behold and everyone is enthralled. The roaring bonfire is well lit now and it is so hot we have to stand really far back. We are waiting on the next part of the fun and that is when the guy starts to burn fiercely and eventually falls off the top or disappears down inside the bonfire. As we all stood there with faces glowing from the light of the fire, the squibs Tam had hidden in the guys pockets ignited with several loud bangs which we were not expecting, this all added to the fun and delight. Little did we know that Tam has hidden a few rockets further over in the sanny hole and he now runs round and sets them all off, much to the delight of everyone at the fire and all the people hanging out the back windows of their houses. Several minutes later, after the rockets are all spent, "Hurrah" a huge cheer goes up again from everyone, as with sparks flying high into the sky, the guy finally gives up his perch on top and crashes down into the middle of the inferno, never to be seen again.

The bonfire burning fiercely, is still standing two hours later, testimony to the thick logs we had used to build it.

The "roastit tatties" we were expecting to cook on the bonfire will not be cooked tonight as the fire is much too hot and the tatties will have to wait until another day.

Mrs Brown sends over some candy apples and tablet she had made earlier saying thanks to us all having helped to clear out her coal house when we were looking for old papers from her.

Candy apples, tablet and a huge bag of monkey nuts that someone else had given us. We were in clover. Not to forget the huge bag of broken biscuits Jenne had given me earlier when I called into the bakers on my way home from school. We sat on the log and devoured this feast while looking at the fire. Most of the crowd had drifted away home now, only myself, Tam, our Sanny, and three of my sisters, Senga, Claire and Jinty with a few of the older kids in the street, were left at the fire.

As it was getting really late now my sisters and our Sanny were about to go home when, with a huge roar, the bonfire crashed in upon itself sending sparks once more high up into the night sky. The fire was reduced to a huge glowing circle of flames on the ground now. Superb, it had been a great night and we were all getting tired now. Dirty and smelling of smoke we trudged up the stairs to the house to get washed and ready for bed. No need for supper tonight as we had gorged ourselves on the goodies we had been given from Jenne and the kindly neighbours.

Oh dear, school tomorrow.

Chapter 8

I have a paper round.

Go tell it on the mountain.

Back in school again. On a Monday morning there is a queue in front of class to put money in the bank. Ever since starting school we were offered an account in the school bank. We never had any money to put in the bank but on this occasion I had sixpence. Standing there, a boy from the toffs houses turned to me and asked, "How much are you putting in the bank?"

I proudly showed him my nice, shiny, sixpenny piece. Then, he said nastily. "A waste of time." As he showed me his half crown.

Leaving the queue with a red face, I sat down and never ever attempted to put any money in the school bank again. This experience of snobbery did sometimes put me off Primary school.

One other demeaning incident at school that stands out in my mind is the time we were practising singing in class and being tested for the school choir. Baa, baa, black sheep was the song. As usual, I was belting out the song with gusto, like in Sunday school or church. Mrs Macleod stopped the class singing and said to me,

"That is enough from you McClure, just mouth the words from now on as you are putting the class off with your tuneless singing."

Horrified and embarrassed and with my singing career in tatters I could not wait to get over the wall to the sanny hole and out of there.

Nevertheless, I did knuckle down and try my best with the other work in school. The same teacher had given me a toy car as a prize for winning the class spelling competition earlier in the year.

Tomorrow before we break up for the holidays there is a Pantomime at the school. RumpelStiltskin is the name. Never having been to a pantomime I was willing to give it the benefit of the doubt.

Four classes at a time are seated cross legged on the drill hall floor. A stage has been set up at one side with tall curtains. The lights are dimmed and all of a sudden the curtains open to reveal the silliest scenery I have ever seen. Cloth trees, cloth grasses with lights that were obvious behind them for effect. I am not impressed. Suddenly a tall stupid looking man appeared jumping about the stage, shouting and bawling at the top of his voice.

"Hello, boys and girls." he said.

"Hello to you." we chorused.

"Behind you," we all shouted, as a strange creature crept up on him.

Five minutes later I had heard enough, my ears were sore listening to him. Quietly I made my way to the toilets and waited, hoping to be here until the whole fiasco was finished. While I was there a man in a bumblebee costume came in for a drink of water. He stared at me after his drink then suddenly he just buzzed off.

Nobody missed me at the pantomime, so I quietly sneaked back to class after it was all over. My friend Bob said they were going to be asking questions about Rumpelstiltskin later. Worrying all that day in case they asked questions, I kept my head down. Bob was holding his sides with laughter when I looked at him and I realised he had been winding me up. Good one Bob.

One of my pals in the street, Walter Sneddon, is giving up his paper round and I am going with him for a week to learn the round and to let him introduce me to the old ladies who own Pettigrews paper shop near the fountain on Sunnyside Road. Monday to Friday I will be delivering evening papers to about twelve to fifteen customers who are scattered over a wide area from Blair Road to Townhead Road and Lomond Road. Saturday and Sunday I will be delivering morning papers to all of the above customers and many more added on.

At the end of that week, Walter gave me half a crown out of his wages as my pay for helping him. At ten years of age this was great. Next week I am on my own and on full pay, which I do not know what that is yet.

On Monday after school I went to the shop only to be told that the evening papers had not arrived from the printers. Would I mind going round the corner to Grant's furniture shop at the fountain and pick the two bundles of papers up when the van drops them off. Round the corner I go to Grants where there are a few of the street newspaper vendors waiting on the van.

A van pulls up at the kerb and a wee square man as broad as he is long, with bow legs, jumps out and runs round to the back door of the van and begins heaving large bundles of Evening Times and Citizen newspapers onto the pavement. All the while he is shouting names and with a rollup cigarette bobbing up and down, stuck to his bottom lip. "Baxter, Jamesy, Coulter, Pettigrew." Oh!!! Pettigrew, that must be one of my bundles. I joined the melee to get the papers and I could not believe the weight of the bundle I had to carry back round to the shop. Struggling into the shop, I lift the bundle on to the counter and go back round for the other one which is equally as heavy.

Waiting patiently until the ladies have my papers ready to deliver, I browse the comics on display on the back wall of the shop. Superman, Commando, Hornet and Hotspur are only a few of the comics here. Making a mental note for pay day, I lift my papers and go for the bus that will take me to my first delivery which is on Blair Road. Then, a long long walk to the second one. The rest of the round is straight forward so I am soon home for supper.

The week went well. Saturday morning I am up and away to get my morning papers on my bike. The shop is quiet and I do not have to wait. The ladies have the papers in order for my round and they have a list of customers who have to pay. No paper for Blair Road at the weekend so this makes the first part of the round simple. Delivering the papers is easy although knocking the doors of people who have to pay slows me down. After getting a few three-penny bits as a tip I have no complaint waiting on people coming to the door to pay. In fact, I have learned to knock on the doors of people who don't need to pay me and this also generates a few tips. I have this job off to a tee I am thinking.

Not so on Sunday morning. It's raining and blowing a gale when I set off to the shop on my bike. The shop is even more quiet so the wee ladies are up for a chat after I have given them the cash I collected yesterday. £12 10/6 was the total. Some customers pay in the shop so I do not need to collect from them all. Sunday papers are much thicker than evening papers, they also have magazines inside them. This makes the bag very heavy indeed. The ladies see me outside the shop struggling to get the bag of papers and myself on to the bike. They call me back in and give me a piece of rope to help tie the bag on to the front. They know that my first stop will be to deliver a few large bundles of papers to customers who live close together and then I will be able to get the bag on my back and mount the bike.

My last delivery on a Sunday is along Wilton Street to the Heather Bell level crossing. Crossing over the railway line always makes me wary so I look both ways and cross over when it is clear to do so. Just a few yards across the line I turn right on the bike down a leafy lane under a canopy of trees and about two hundred yards to a little ivy-covered cottage nestling in the trees. Normally Walter and I had run along the railway line to the level crossing as he did not have a bike. A little old lady takes me into the house and makes me stand in front of the open range fire for a heat and to get dry. An old man sitting on one side of the fire smoking a clay pipe, asks me, "Whose father are you then?"

I say, "I am too young to be anyone's father yet."

"Correct answer son," he replied. "Who is your father then?"

Ach, leave the laddie alone," says the old woman.

"Am only teasing him," the old man says.

"Well it's time for him to go," she said, as she ushered me to the door.

"Thanks for the heat," I said to the old lady.

"No bother son, we will see you next week." Handing me a threepenny bit for a tip. The Heather Bell gates are open and I pedal furiously to get over the level crossing before the barrier comes down. A few minutes later I hear the bell signalling the gates are coming down and a train is coming. Pedalling as fast as I can, I can't wait to get home and count my tips. The tips I have amount to 3 shillings and 9 pence, 3\9d. Taking out my pay envelope I show Mam the money I got paid today 12/6 and I give it to her, as I know she needs it.

"Thanks laddie, you know I will use it wisely." She says, smiling. Happy with my own tip money I go to my room and plank the money under my bed. The time is still only 10 a.m so the rest of the household is getting up now for breakfast. As I have been round the town on my bike on my paper round, mam says I don't need to go to church and just to stay in and have a rest. Our Sanny says he wants to come with me next week as he thinks it will get him out of going to church.

On occasion Sanny does come with me on a Saturday and a Sunday to help get the papers delivered quicker and it is great for me to have his company. Sanny gets 6d from me for helping out so he is happy with that.

Chapter 9

Easter Sunday.

Rolled away, Rolled away,
The burden on my heart
Rolled away.

A nice sunny Easter morning and I am still up early to go and do my paper round. Going into the shop the wee Pettigrew ladies are very cheery and they have my papers all ready for me.

"Happy Easter, Davie," they chorus.

"Happy Easter, ladies," I say, and they giggle at that.

Once our monetary business is complete and the bike is loaded with the Sunday papers, the ladies, smiling broadly, give me a large smarties chocolate Easter egg and say again.

"Happy Easter, Davie."

"Thank you very much ladies."

Giggling again like teenagers, they ask me where our Sanny is this morning.

"Och, he is having a long lie because of the Easter weekend holiday," I reply.

"Well, there you go, here is another Easter egg for him, from us." I could not thank them enough for the eggs and made to leave the shop when one of the ladies asked me,

"Do you have any other brothers? "

I replied, "Yes, I have another two brothers."

Another two chocolate button eggs in a box appeared from below the counter.

"There you go Davie. Give them these eggs from us."

I am starting to feel embarrassed now and can't wait to get out of the shop when the other wee lady asks me the killer question.

"Davie, do you have any sisters?"

Well!! I did not know where to look, I could feel my face go red with embarrassment, when I said, "I have seven sisters."

Both of the ladies' facial expressions changed from smiling, to surprise then shock, or maybe even horror. I was not sure. Nevertheless, the two of them went through to the back shop and opened up a large cardboard box of eggs and brought seven more boxed eggs out to me at the front of the shop. Despite my protestations when I was saying that myself and my brothers would share our eggs with my sisters, they insisted on giving me another newspaper delivery bag for all eleven large boxed Easter eggs. Really struggling now to get on the bike, I was still outside the shop when I could hear one of the sisters saying to the other,

"Well!! That was a costly exercise this morning."

The other sister laughed.

"Well, you asked him the questions, and anyway, we wouldn't sell any more eggs after today so this is a great way to give a nice family a good Easter and wee Davie is a good dependable boy."

Beaming with pride I decided it was easier to walk home and balance the two large newspaper bags on the bike. I set off feeling very proud of myself after hearing all the nice things the ladies had said.

Some of my customers got their papers on time but, as I passed my house, I went in with the Easter eggs. My brothers and sisters were just getting up for breakfast when I arrived home with the goodies. Gathering mam and my brothers and sisters in the living room to show them the huge bag in the middle of the floor, they do not know that it is full of boxed chocolate eggs. Everyone is excited to see what is in the bag. I invite them all to come forward and reach into the bag and pick one. Everyone comes forward to pick an egg out of the bag and they are all sitting grinning with their eggs. There is one left in the bottom of the bag, which I give to Mam, as my wee sister Lucy is still in her pram and too young to get one. Everyone was sitting enthralled as I was explaining how I had ended up with all these eggs. Telling them of the happy wee ladies, then the glum wee ladies and finally the happy wee ladies again as I set off struggling with my load. What a brilliant time we had, all before breakfast.

Mam said to our Sanny, "Hurry up and help David with the rest of his paper round and I will have a big breakfast ready for you when you come back."

Sanny was happy to help me and we set off to deliver the papers, albeit a little later than normal. Nobody complained and we got more tips as it was Easter weekend. Sanny got a shilling from me for his efforts so he was happy.

Up the road, as we used to say, then into the house for breakfast. Mam put the breakfast down on the scullery table and we tucked in to slice sausage, bacon and eggs with fried bread.

After breakfast Mam showed us a pot with a dozen hard boiled eggs in it. Some were really brown as they had been boiled in the teapot with tea leaves and the others were pale as they had been boiled with plain water. She said, "This is a job for later, you can all paint these eggs with your coloured pencils or paints and then when they are done, we are all going to the daisy park for a picnic in the afternoon and you can all roll your eggs."

The daisy park is a ten to fifteen minute walk away up the Blair Road. As it is such a nice day it will be very busy.

On the way to the park Sanny, Senga and I scoffed our boiled eggs because we did not want to roll them and get them dirty. That was our excuse anyway.

We had a shawl with us to spread on the grass and we set up our own picnic area. Lucy, my youngest sister's pram, was handy for carrying all the stuff we needed with us. Boiled eggs, chocolate eggs, sandwiches and diluting juice made up in a large jug and some Creamola Foam mixed in water. A feast indeed. Children were running all over the place and enjoying playing chasing games like "tig," or they were running in races organised by some of the parents. Rolling the boiled eggs ended up messy at times as some people had not hard boiled their eggs.

The girls were all making daisy chains from the daisies they had picked. After an hour or so we were all settled down on the grass, tired and puffed out with all the exertion. The bags were opened and out came the food. There was silence as everybody tucked into the picnic.

Soon it was time to go home and we all trekked wearily up the road. Another great day had by all.

Chapter 10

An afternoon at the coup.

All things bright and beautiful

School is out early on a Friday so my school pal Bob has convinced me to go along with him to the coup, where all the town's rubbish is dumped. Never having been there before, I am asking him loads of questions about why we should go there. Bob says there is great stuff to be had at the coup as not everything people throw away is useless. Bob knows the man who drives the bulldozer levelling out all the rubbish tipped from the constant stream of bin lorries that arrive.

Bob waves as he passes and the driver waves back at us. Turns out, the driver is the father of one of the girls in our class at school. We skirt around the edge of the coup for a while until the bulldozer comes rumbling over to us and the driver stops and jumps out and says "Hi " to Bob.

"Who is your pal then?" He says.

This is Davie, he is in my school class." Bob tells him.

"OK then boys, jump into the bulldozer and I will take you over to where the best stuff is today."

We climb into the bulldozer cab and he climbs in beside us and starts the engine. What a feeling of power underneath us as the engine roars into life and the exhaust spouts black smoke then turning white.

Trundling to the other side of the coup away from the bin lorries coming in, the bulldozer driver takes us to a part of the coup that he says will be full of good stuff as the lorries that had come in there in the morning, were bringing stuff from the posh houses in Langloan, Blairhill and Drumpellier. Before he drove away he shouted down to us that if we did find any gold then it was his. Off went the bulldozer with a roar again and with a big smile on his face, the driver waved to us.

Bob and I set to work raking for good stuff. Sure enough there were a lot of items that were not broken and not all the rubbish was wet and stinking. The best stuff we found was in bags and we were able to gather quite a pile that looked like we could take some of it home.

Unaffordable to us, some books, annuals and magazines were treasures that we gathered, along with a set of good pram wheels that we would use to cart our finds home. We waved to the bulldozer driver as we were leaving and he stopped to make sure we left safely. As I had further to go home I was getting to keep the pram wheels. We got to Bob's house and I helped him in with his goodies.

Bob's father and older brothers were pigeon men and he took me down to meet them in the back garden where there was a large square shed called a "dooket" or dovecot, with a landing stage for pigeons on one side. The pigeons are all in the air together flying away from us when one of Bob's brothers lets out a shrill whistle and they wheel round together and fly back towards us.

This is an amazing display and we stood there for half an hour watching. It is getting dark now so I need to go home. Grabbing the set of pram wheels with the goodies on and running up the street towards the roundabout I am already planning my new "bogie."

Most of what I bring home from the coup is put to the side and used for fuel for the fire. Some of the books and magazines keep us reading quietly at night for a few days. My sisters get to look at the fashion catalogues of clothes and household goods I had brought home also. Catalogues full of stuff we could not afford.

Uncle Johnny came to visit us one Saturday to tell us he was going away to work abroad for a long time. He had recently worked in Rhodesia (now Zambia) in Africa, building the Kariba dam hydro electric scheme for two years. This time he was going to Thailand for three years. We could not believe it, we would all miss him. Uncle Johnny was always laughing and full of fun. He was also very generous when he came to visit. Doling out half crowns to us, we were rich for a short time until Mam promptly collected the money after he left.

Uncle Johnny always had new sayings for us to remember. "Scumficed" was one. This was a saying he had when someone had broken wind on a bus or a train. He would say he was "scumficed" instead of stunk out. "Kipper hups" was another saying he had.

There is a story in the family about Uncle Johnny taking one of his nephews out to Whifflet for a treat. On the return journey the nephew was taken short with diarrhea. (plastered was the description we heard). Already sitting comfortably on the bus to go home with his nephew when the conductress saw and smelled the predicament and ejected them both from the bus with a few choice words. The nephew since then has lovingly been known as "Whifflet hups."

Always very polite spoken, Uncle Johnny was nearly home from the pub one night when he met a neighbour out walking her dog. He said to her, "Good evening madam, how are you and how is your stinking dog?"

The neighbour said to him.

"My dog is not stinking and I will tell your mother about all this cheek from you in the morning."

Uncle Johnny laughed at her and was amazed that this woman would threaten him with his Mammy. He was thirty five years old, for goodness sake.

Uncle Johnny had a glass eye which made him more fascinating to us. We all loved him.

Having one eye prevented Uncle Johnny from joining the forces like his brothers during the second World war. Nevertheless, the home guard was delighted to have him. They inducted him and told him he had no choice but to do the training as the town needed protection from invaders.

Uncle Johnny would be out on firewatch or marching with the wooden rifle over his shoulder at night. He would find good reasons to slow down on the march and park the wooden gun against the railings at Drumpellier Primary school and cross the road to The Angus Bar pub when nobody was watching. We are sure he thought the town was probably safer without his marching and his wooden rifle. We are all going to miss him when he goes on his travels again.

Chapter 11

A visit to the canal.

We will gather at the river.

Tam and I, along with two of his brothers, are going over the Blair Road to the Monklands canal.

This disused canal was very busy at one time, stretching from Airdrie or just beyond, through Coatbridge and into Glasgow. Horse drawn barges were used on the canal to ferry coal and other goods to different places along the way. Tam had heard there was a large raft floating under the Blair Road bridge so he wanted us to find it and go for a sail down the canal.

When we got there, the makeshift raft was upside down with huge nails sticking out of it. We tried unsuccessfully to turn it over but to no avail. We walked along under the Blair Road bridge to a concrete area on the towpath just behind Smiths garage and across from the plots. This area looked like a landing stage.

We decided to sit down here and dangle our feet in the water but that was never going to be enough. Stripping off to his underpants, Tam was first into the canal and swimming about, both of his brothers did not hesitate and were quickly in behind him. Tentatively, I followed suit and quickly joined the melee in the middle of the canal. Touching the silt on the bottom of the canal with my feet felt all squidgy and horrible. After fifteen minutes or so, we were starting to get cold and the water was turning a horrible grey brownish colour with us stirring up the sediment on the bottom. An old woman walking past told us that a couple of dead dogs were seen floating in there last week and we might have caught a horrible disease from the putrid water. We needed no more prompting and we scrambled out of the water quickly. We ran about to get dry before getting dressed, pretending to try and throw each other back in the water.

Enough was enough, we headed back up the Blair Road and as we passed the plots we went in to see some of the gardeners. I had been here before and knew where to go to find a friendly man who would sell us some fruit and veg. We walked past some rather grumpy looking men tending their plants. Little did we know that some boys had come in a few days before and vandalised some of the plots so they were not very welcoming. We reached the plot where Mr Potts was sitting on an old wooden box smoking his pipe.

"Well Davie, what can I do you for today?"

I replied. "We are not here to be done Mr Potts, but we would like to buy some rhubarb and tomatoes from you."

We had pooled our resources for this and had scraped together fourpence which we handed to Mr Potts. He looked at the money then handed it back to us.

"Tell your oul man I was asking for him." Said Mr Potts, as he gave us a huge armful of rhubarb and a bag of big tomatoes.

We left the plots and hurried home with the goodies. We shared the bundle of rhubarb between us and I finished up with the tomatoes as Tam and his brother did not like them.

Mam was delighted with all of this and gave me back a thick stalk of rhubarb and a small bag of sugar to dip in. Mam made a large rhubarb pie that day and my wee brothers and sisters got some rhubarb and sugar dips too. Mam said to me that it had not gone unnoticed that once again I did not look dirty or clean so I must have been in the canal. Before she could say any more I promised not to go in there again and I never did.

Another good day and that night, once more, into the land of nod, I slept like a log.

Chapter 12

Summary holiday at the farm

Bringing in the sheaves, bringing in the sheaves
We will gather joyfully, bringing in the sheaves.

The whole household is buzzing with excitement this morning. School broke up yesterday for an eight weeks summer holiday. Claire, Jinty, Senga, our Sanny and I are getting ready to go to Aberdeenshire to my granny's farm for eight weeks.

This trip is huge for all of us. Mam talks to us often of the good times that she had while growing up in rural Aberdeenshire. Up early to feed the hens, collect eggs and feed the dogs.

We cannot wait to go. Claire, Jinty and I have been at the farm before.

Last night my sisters had a home perm and our Sanny says they are looking rather sheepish with their tight curls. Senga did not need a perm as she has blonde curly hair anyway. The night before was hilarious as we watched them getting their pipe cleaners in their hair and a stinking pee smelling potion clarted on their heads to make the tight curls.

Sanny and I had been to McLays the barber at Sunnyside this morning for a haircut. There are six barbers there so we know we will not need to wait long for our turn. We watch all the barbers cutting hair with the scissors still snipping and snapping away in their hand, even when no hair is being cut. Sanny is up on the chair first and the barber needs to put a plank of wood across the arms of the chair as he is so short.

"What would you like today sir?" says the barber.

Sanny tells him, "A short back and sides with plinty off the top Mam says."

The barber looks round to me for confirmation and I point to a picture on the wall of an American GI with a crew cut.

"OK," says the barber. "What mam wants is what mam gets."

So, away goes the barber with scissors clack clack clacking and proceeds to give Sanny a crew cut. Sanny knows not to move a muscle while on the chair as I have warned him, if he does, he may be in danger of having his lug snipped off. I get exactly the same haircut.

Walking home together, Sanny is patting my crew cut and I am patting his crew cut, he says to me,

"What do you think mam will say about this?" I say to him.

"I do not have a clue Sanny, maybe she will not be happy." Knowing full well that mam told me to get us a crew cut.

Am thinking that our haircuts go well with the new American style baseball boots we have on. Baseball boots are even better than new sannies for running.

Running like mad the two of us are desperate to get home. Not before we go to the baker's first. Up Gartsherrie Road we run, getting nearer our destination. On the way back to the house, we stop off into the bakers to let Jenne know we are going away for all of the school holidays so she will not see us for a while. Jenne stands us up against the back wall of the shop for inspection.

"How very smart and clean you both look today boys, I know that you will all have a good time at the farm and your mam will get a rest at home while you are all away too." With a wink at us she said, "Here is a bag of special broken biscuits for your journey."

We both thank Jenne very much and run all the rest of the way home. Looking inside the bag, mam discovers there are not many broken biscuits but a whole lot of unbroken chocolate biscuits and some cakes too. Mam knows Jenne very well and really appreciates and values her friendship. As do we.

We can't wait to get going on our holiday now.

We say our goodbyes to mam and the rest of the family and dressed in our best clothes we walk up the Avenue to the bus stop on Lomond Road. The blue double decker Baxter's bus will take us to the fountain at Coatbridge town centre. From there we can walk round the corner to the Central station. Central station is quite busy today with lots of other people going on holiday. The oul man who is carrying the case is taking us to the station to get the tickets and see us off on our journey to Aberdeen. One big case is enough for our holiday clothes for eight weeks as we will all get kitted out with farm clothes and wellies when we get there.

Walking into the station we can see the long train standing at Platform 1 and the huge steam engine at the front is spitting steam now and again from the pistons. While the oul man buys our return tickets, I go up the plat-form to look at the massive steam engine that is going to pull these eight carriages all the way to Aberdeen. This engine is a monster compared to the PUG steam engine I had driven in the oul man's work. I absolutely love it.

"Come on David." Chorused my brother and sisters,

"We are getting on the train now."

I wave to the driver and his fireman, both of whom are leaning out of the cab watching me. They give me a wave with their bunnets and tell me,

"You better get going son, we are leaving soon."

Running back down the platform I get on the train, and along the corridor following everyone else into a compartment, which will be our own for the four and a half hour journey. The large case is put high up in a net type shelf above our heads. There is a table in the middle at the window with a long platform style cushioned seat down each side. Our Sanny, Senga and I are at one side of the table with my older sisters Claire and Jinty at the other side. We have a piece bag each in a bigger bag on the table, full of goodies to eat on the journey. The oul man gives Claire, who is twelve, all of the tickets to look after and puts Jinty in charge of the pieces. We all have some money in our pockets to buy soft drinks from the buffet car. Claire has been given instructions on what we all have to do to be safe.

The choice of compartment is near a toilet so we do not need to go far. The carriage in front of ours is the buffet car so we do not have far to go for a drink either. We have been suitably settled on the train in our own compartment so the oul man gets off and onto the platform to wave us away. Slam, Slam, Slam, we hear the guard slamming the carriage doors as he walks down the platform from the front to the rear of the train where he jumps into the Guards van and takes up his position. The guard hangs out the window blowing his whistle and waving a green flag to the driver who is a long way down at the front. The driver pulls the cord which blows the train's steam whistle. "Phweet, Phweet, Phweet," and we are off on the first leg of our journey. We keep waving frantically to the oul man as we slowly move away round the curve of the platform until we can no longer see him.

The train passes a lot of familiar places to us and we eagerly point out to each other, landmarks that we know. Gartsherrie iron works, Sunnyside canal basin, where the long coal barges are turned around. Lambertons Engineering, the Gas works. We pass Northburn and Waverley steel works out towards Kipps farm and then we are in the countryside.

Gradually the train gathers speed as it heads North out of the town and we no longer recognise anywhere, so we settle down to look out the window for a while and listen to the music of the train wheels as they pass over joints and points on the track.

"Fiddle de dee, Fiddle de dah, fiddle de diddle de dah." The train sings to us as we sit quietly looking at the countryside flashing by.

After a while we get out some paper and pencils we have and play some word games to pass the time. We have instructions to all sing loudly, if anyone looks as if they are going to come in and occupy the vacant seats we have in our compartment. Only one or two people looked in, but they soon moved on as we belted out an old favourite song.

"Ohh, ye canny shove yer granny aff the bus,
ohh, ye canny shove yer granny aff the bus.
Oh ye canny shove yer granny,
'coz she's yer mammys mammy,
ye canny shove yer granny aff the bus."

This turns out to be a brilliant ploy and we roll about the seats laughing when they move on.

First stop is Stirling, so we look out for the Castle or William Wallace's monument as we slow down coming into the station. Excited to see if we could see the Castle or the monument, we discovered that, as the station is at the other side of the town, we only catch a glimpse of the top of the Castle.

We settled down to watch the coming and goings of people on the platform as the train had a five minute stop.

We are off again, next stop Perth. The train will stop for ten minutes here and we can have our pieces too. Some people get off to walk up and down the platform to stretch their legs. There is a lot of hustle and bustle on the platform with three wheeler railway buggies pulling flatbed bogies full of suitcases up and down. There are tea trolley vendors on the platform selling tea, coffee, sandwiches and cakes. We watch the platform action as we all tuck into our pieces. Claire and Jinty go to the buffet car and bring back glasses of orange juice for us in large thick tumblers. "Phweet phweet." The train whistle sounds, to warn stragglers on the platform to get on the train.

Off we go again, towards Dundee, the next stop.

Crossing the river Tay rail bridge into Dundee is a spectacle to behold. The bridge has a large curve and we can see the engine that is pulling us along. We look out the window down to the river which is far away below us. We tell Sanny and Senga that this is where OOR WULLIE was born. We know that it is the home of DC Thomson, the printer who put Oor Wullie and the Broons into the Sunday Post newspaper. Desperate Dan too, was born here. Suddenly our Sanny stands up on the seat and exclaims,

"That's the emergency brake up there!!" We all look up to the red six inch long chain that is the emergency brake. "PULL HERE." States the sign below the chain. We explain to Sanny that the sign is not an invitation to pull the chain and if he does then we would all be in trouble if there was no emergency and the chain had been pulled. We move Sanny as far away from the chain as possible as he is still eyeing it up. Claire tells me to go to the toilet with Sanny when he is ready, as she is worried that the emergency pull chain is also available in the toilet.

We play some games, like, I spy with my little eye, the minister's cat, also a favourite. The ticket collector had come in after we left Perth to inspect and punch our tickets. Giving Claire the punched tickets back for our return, he said, "Do not lose these tickets hen, if you do, you will need to walk home."

Away he went grinning to himself. Our Senga says,

"As if we would walk all the way home from Aberdeen. Silly sod."

The train passed through Forfar without stopping. We are travelling along the cliffs and we are now able to see the North Sea. No oil rigs out there in those days. We knew it would not be long until we got to Aberdeen.

At last, the train is slowing down as it approaches our destination. We have tidied up any mess we may have made and get ready to depart the train. The train has stopped now so all the doors are being opened and we can all step down onto the platform. Sanny asks Claire,

"Would it be OK to pull the chain now then?" Claire grabs him and hauls him off the train by the scruff of the neck and says to him,

"What planet are you on our Sanny? How can you be so silly wanting to do something like that. You have been told not to do it?"

Sanny went into a wee huff for a while after being chastised.

We have quite a walk to the gate where Aunt Izzie will be waiting for us. Passing the engine that has pulled us all the way here I am disappointed to see that the driver and shunter are not the same two we started off with. Little did I know that there had been a change of driver and shunter at Perth. Undaunted, I shouted up to them and thanked them both for getting us here safely. Looking puzzled and really surprised they told me I was very welcome.

Excited and happy now and, as expected, Aunt Izzie is there waiting with a big smile for us all.

"Weel Weel an, foo are yiz deein?" she asks.

It is good to hear her accent and the Doric that our Mam talks to us all the time.

"Weel, I dinna ken fit yer Mam feeds you lot but yiz are fair grouin," she says.

Trooping along behind her, listening to her chatting to our Claire, we get to the car park and pile into the old Ford ten she is driving.

The last leg of our journey to the farm begins. We are going through the Granite city of Aberdeen very slowly as the traffic is always very busy on a Saturday. As we pass along Union Street we can look down and see people in the park playing outdoor chess and checkers on huge game boards fixed to the ground. Getting out of the city now and up over the ring road towards the airport, the car is travelling a bit faster. Sanny is out of his huff and eagerly trying to spot aeroplanes. In those days an aircraft in the sky was a novelty and people stopped to look as a plane flew past. We go past the road to Clinterty college and over the Tyre-bagger Brae.

As we get over the top of the brae we are all looking eagerly for our first sighting of "Bennachie." We all see it at the same time. "There it is!!" we exclaim. We are filled with emotion as we see it for the first time on this holiday.

Bennachie is a hill in Aberdeenshire that can be seen for many miles all around. The hill reminds us of a volcano and does not look like the rest of the hills in the area which are covered in evergreen conifer trees. Twenty miles and slightly North West from Aberdeen is our grannie's farm, titled (Mains of Afforsk) which is nestling just one or two miles to the South side of Benachie.

Passing through small towns and villages with great sounding names to us, Bucksburn, Kintore, Monymusk, Kemnay, Fetternear and Inverurie are only a few of the names familiar to us older ones in the car. Blairdaff is one of the villages that has a church and only one shop which usually serves as the Post Office and the Petrol Station.

A few miles from Blairdaff we turn left off the main road down the farm track which has grass growing in the middle. Looking straight down the road we can see in the distance that at one time the track had gone half way up the Millstone hill but is now mainly overgrown. As we travel slowly down the rough track we can see ahead of us the hills all covered in conifers. Half a mile down the track to the right is the farmhouse that we will call home for the next eight weeks. We can only see the roof of the house as it is surrounded by lots of different types of trees. Turning right, up past the garden and right again into what they call the close.

We have arrived.

We call granny, "Benachie mam" for obvious reasons and our grandad is called Donal. When we arrive at the farm we all pile out Aunt Izzies car to be greeted by

"Benachie mam" who is a small happy looking rotund woman with a wraparound pinnie on. Aunt Izzie's son, our cousin Harry who lives there most of the time, is waiting too. We are so excited to get into the house and get into old clothes that we forget to give Bennachie mam a hug. She calls us back and one by one we are inspected, then, with a big smile, we are hugged and patted on the head.

Suitably approved, welcomed and patted on the head we are told to go into the kitchen as we are going to get our denner noo. We all troop through the porch which is the rear entrance to the Farmhouse. The whole downstairs of the house is stone floored with an occasional rug here and there.

We hang up our coats and jackets in the lobby which is, ben the hoose. Meanwhile Aunt Izzie takes our case upstairs.

Into the large kitchen we go where there is a huge open cooking range with all sorts of pots bubbling away on top. The long kitchen table is at the window on the right hand side with a wooden bench to sit on at each side. On the left hand side of the range, in the corner, is an ancient armchair where Donal is sitting quietly, with his bunnet on and smoking his pipe. Donal is our grandad, he has a very weather beaten face and is quite a small wiry looking man with no teeth. He gives us a similar welcome to Benachie mam and is shaking hands with us boys (his hands feel like leather) then playfully pretending that he does not like girls on his farm as they are ah eesless. (All useless.)

With Donal now sitting at the end of the table with his bunnet off, we settle down as Benachie mam and Aunt Izzie, who are chattering away in The Doric, busy them-selves getting dinner out.

We have a large bowl of homemade soup first, then we lick the plate, then onto the same plate go the potatoes with cushie doo (wood pigeon) and peas. We have been here before and we all know what to expect. The cushie doo is great and we all get a whole one each. Plates all licked clean again, there is sago pudding to finish, with a big dollop of homemade raspberry jam in the middle. Suitably stuffed, we cannot move after such a large meal.

Donal is back in his ancient armchair filling his pipe with bogey roll. Then he asks us all individually how well we are doing at the skweel. (School) He wants a reminder of what age and height we are. We are made to stand up and he feels our biceps to see if we are fit for work. This is all jokingly and cheerfully done, pretending to see if we are fit to earn our keep. Cousin Harry is included in this too. Meanwhile, Claire and Jinty are both clearing up the table and the dishes to help Bennachie mam.

Our Sanny who is not backward at asking a personal question asks Donal where his teeth are. Donal, pretending to look shocked, takes his teeth out of his jacket pocket and shows them to us. (not a pretty sight).

"What do you think of them clackers then?" He said, with a big toothless grin. Sanny then has to ask him

"Why do you not put them in your mouth for your dinner, Donal?" Donal says to him,

"I will tell you what I tellt the Dentist when he asked me the same question. These teeth are nae ees for eatin, but they are grand drinkers."

With a big toothless grin, then putting his bottom lip over his nose and looking like popeye, Donal put the teeth back in his jacket pocket. Sanny is not finished with him yet, he then asks Donal, "So, is that why you didn't have any tatties with your dinner then?"

"Never liked tatties and av never eaten een. Next question, Sanny?" he says.

Sanny says, "That is enough for me today unless anyone else wants to ask him something."

We all look at each other but we have no more questions for Donal.

A farmer who does not like tatties!! We find this very hard to believe but, over the years and many visits to the farm we never ever saw Donal eat a tattie.

Aunt Izzie and Benachie mam are both quite small and look almost identical. In fact, they both look, not surprisingly, like our Mam, although Mam is a little taller. They even have a woolly headed perm like my sisters. This must be the latest fashion thing. Listening to the chatter in the kitchen we can see and hear where mam gets all her sayings from.

They are both interested to know how the rest of the family are doing so Claire and Jinty fill them in on what is happening at home. Meanwhile, Sanny, Senga and I leave Donal to his teeth, gums and pipe and cannot wait to get out and about the farm to look at the tractors, lorries and the new bulldozer that Donal has acquired since our holiday here last year.

As we step out of the door we can see Benachie hill looming closer now and not so far in the distance. This is the view we get every time we leave the house. Benachie Hill, strangely, we are told, has some control of what happens on the farm. Donal explained this by telling us, if you can see Benachie clearly, then the weather is fine and you can work. If you cannot see it completely clearly then it is going to rain so prepare to stop work. If you cannot see it at all, then it is raining heavily and there will be no work today. After this explanation we would be asked when we went into the house.

"What is Benachie saying noo then?"

Knowing we would be asked this question when going into the house we always looked at the hill first for the answer.

Off we go out with cousin Harry to have a look round. Harry is very keen to show us everything there is on the farm as this is his domain. During the tour of the farm Harry is at pains to let us know that he is in charge even though he is only ten years old. Sanny and I know that Harry is a bit spoiled and maybe he felt a bit threatened when we all descended earlier, so we let him think we will let him be in charge of us, knowing full well we will do what we like when we like, within reason.

Our Sanny needs the toilet so I tell him what I told him earlier about where and what it is.

The dry toilet is half way down the left side of the garden. It is a little narrow wooden shed, under a large holly tree. The door has a little diamond cut in it to allow light in as there are no windows. There is no lock on the door, so, When you sit down to do your business you have to put your foot on the door to keep it closed. Anyway, Sanny has a look inside to see this wooden bench with a round hole in the middle. Below the hole is a large bucket that is full to the top with papers and other people's business. Sanny runs out holding his nose and making retching and vomiting noises.

"No way am I going to ever use that toilet, what is that all about?"

I explained to him that it is called a dry toilet and it needs to be emptied and cleaned regularly. There is no sanitation in the house and they have only recently got running water into the sink.

"What am I going to do then? "He asks.

"Back of a tree," I told him,"back of a tree."

Away I go again, laughing all the way. Later on, Sanny asks me, "Why the back of a tree?"

I tell him, "Nobody would ever go at the front of a tree, Would they?"

Happy with that answer Sanny runs off to play.

I have yet to explain to Sanny what the pail under the bed is for. Bearing in mind we are going to be sleeping on a mattress on the floor so there is no under our bed.

Tired after all the excitement of the day and our long journey, we are ready for bed that night by nine o clock. Not before Benachie mam gives us all a piece with home-made jam, or a biscuit, or something else along with a hot chocolate drink. Claire and Jinty have been upstairs earlier with Aunt Izzie to sort out our sleeping arrangements. Donal tells us to go up and get into bed quickly when we finish oor teh, as he will be going out soon to the kert shed to switch off the generator that gives us electric light.

The generator has been an addition since we were last here. We used to sit beside the range fire at night by the light of a "Tilley paraffin lamp" and listen to Donal's funny stories. Then we would go to bed by the light of a torch. Great times then, although the electric light we have now, is a great luxury. Lying in bed we can hear Donal's tacketty boots clumping out of the porch and along the close to the kert shed to switch off the generator. The lights in the house start to dull down as the generator slows and stops. Then, we can hear Donal's tacketty boots coming back across the cobbles, echoing in the dark. We settle down to sleep at the end of what has been a really exciting and tiring day. We can hear an owl hooting in the distance, a lost lamb bleating for it's mother too and the occasional moo from a cow. As darkness falls we drift off into the land of nod once again.

Morning has broken as they say, a cockerel is crowing far away in the distance, bright sunlight is streaming in the skylight window. We have no option but to get up. Sanny and I, sitting on the mattress on the floor, survey our surroundings in this long bedroom upstairs. The ceiling is sloping, hence the skylight. There is a single bed at the far end of the room where our Senga is still sleeping. Sanny and I have been lying on a very comfortable double mattress on the floor at the other side. There is a large sideboard and dressing table in the room also. Claire and Jinty slept in a double bed in the room at the other side of the top landing. Sanny and I get quietly dressed in the old clothes provided for farm living, then, we playfully give Senga a real solid pummeling with our pillows to get her wakened then run quickly down the wooden spiral staircase before she gathers her senses, as we know, she is well able to fight us back, hard.

Donal is in his chair filling his pipe while Bennachie mam is busy at the range and she says "Weel, weel boys you are just in time for your brose, did you sleep OK?"

"Oh aye, we had a great sleep," we both said.

We slide in behind the table at the window and we are served our brose in a wooden bowl with a jug of milk to help ourselves from. The three girls come downstairs and sit on the other bench waiting for their breakfast.

Senga is looking daggers at us so we just grin back at her, innocently. Our sister is a bit of a Tomboy and we are sure she will have her revenge, in some shape or form. A bowl of brose and milk followed by a large boiled egg and toast for each of us, we feel spoiled again. Our Sanny spies the double barreled shotgun and the .22 rifle leaning on the wall behind Donals chair so he asks when he can get a shot. Donal brings out the guns and stands them up next to Sanny and he says to him.

"When you are taller than these twa guns you can get a shot."

Sanny has quite a few inches to go so he will not get a shot any time soon. "Until then you must never touch them." He is told by Donal.

Satisfied with that answer, Sanny goes off to wash himself in the sink in the porch which only has cold water. I join him, gingerly putting the freezing water on our faces. We are both washed now and dry ourselves off with the towel that is hanging on the big nail behind the porch door. We look out the door first then go back in and tell everyone that Benachie says it will be a good working day today. Donal and Benachie mam look at each other and smile at that. The girls stay in the kitchen to help Benachie mam clear up so Sanny and I go outside to see what is happening elsewhere.

Senga knows the morning pummeling will be a daily occurrence if she does nothing about it, so she tells Benachie mam. Armed with this information Benachie mam gives Sanny and I a good telling off when we are in for lunch later. "If you burst those pillows you will have none for the rest of your holiday so think aboot it."

We are both apologising profusely saying,

"It won't happen again."

Senga was grinning in the corner while we were being chastised and if I am correct, Benachie mam was having a quiet smile to herself too.

Back outside we are standing admiring the view of Benachie hill in the distance when we hear a commotion in the hen hoose. Cousin Harry who was up and fed way before the rest of us is trying to get all the hens outside. We helped him with this by throwing some crusts of bread outside that we had saved from breakfast. All the hens run outside for the crusts and Harry can now gather the eggs from all the boxes. Harry has a wicker basket that is pretty full of eggs after five minutes. We go and get another one to help him. Looking in all the wee nooks and crannies, inside and outside and under the hedges too. All the eggs we can find are now safely collected and taken into the scullery to be washed and graded for the butcher who is coming later this afternoon.

Sanny and I go out and get a pail to fill up from the corn loft to feed the hens. A long trail of hens are running after us as we go to the wooden trough at the side of the hen hoose and spread the corn from one end to the other. The hens are lined up on both sides of the trough pecking away furiously.

Finished with that task we go to look for something else to do. A couple of ducks are having a drink out of the horse trough, so we put some bruised corn down, which is better for them.

We go to explore in the byre but before we get there we hear loud grunting in one of the sheds. On opening the half door we look over and lo and behold, inside, is a massive boar, bigger and longer than any pig we have ever seen. Huge floppy lugs shade his eyes from the glare of the sun as he looks up at us. We asked him.

"What are you looking for today?"

No answer from him but his trough is empty so we go and ask in the house if it is time for him to be fed, if so, what will we give him. Benachie mam says. "Wait till after dinner and I will have a pail of stuff for you then."

Exploring around the farm is great fun as we familiarise ourselves with all the equipment. In the corn yard behind the byre stands the Thrashing Mill. This is a huge piece of mainly wooden machinery that sits on four wheels. It has levers, pulleys, belts and crankshafts going in all directions. There is a huge green hap over the top of the thrashing mill and hanging down both sides we can read the name of the owner.

DONALD MITCHELL
Mains of Afforsk

Donal hires himself out with his thrashing mill all over Aberdeenshire bringing in other farmers' harvest and earning money to invest in the farm. Sometimes, we hear, he is so busy with other farmers' harvest that he is one of the last in the area to bring in his own. If the weather were to turn suddenly wet he would struggle to get his harvest in. Donal is constantly reminded of this fact by Benachie mam, as, like many other farmers wives, she's the boss of the farm at the end of the day.

We would be fascinated to see the mill working but cousin Harry tells us we will all be back at the Skweel before harvest time. Sanny and I are disappointed but there is still lots more to see yet and we know that we will soon be working in the hay fields if the sunny weather continues for a few more days.

Back inside for our lunch we get a large bowl of soup with homemade triangular breid (oatcakes.) Bowls licked clean, then a bowl of sago pudding with raspberry jam. Again. We will soon be fed up with sago pudding. Not to be ungrateful we will all still scoff the sago pudding down.

Benachie mam gives Sanny and I a pail each to take out to the boar. My pail, she says, is full of guts from the six hares she had gutted and prepared this morning for the butcher when he comes later. Sanny's pail was full of hare fur, hare feet and hare heads.

"Give the boar the guts, then go down to the bottom of the wee park and dig a hole and bury the heids, feet and fur."

We both enter the shed gingerly with our pails. The boar is waiting. Holding my pail high and slowly moving the boar over with my knee to get access to the trough I am pouring the guts in when Sanny gives a shout and a scream then climbs up over the half door back outside. His pail is lying on it's side with the boar's snout all the way inside to get the heids, skins and feet out. Sanny did not think to leave his pail outside and as I was moving the boar over it had sniffed out the contents of his pail and knocked it out of his hand. No point in trying to take the skins n heids off the boar now, as it is happily crunching the hare skulls then trying with great difficulty to swallow the dry hare skins down. While it is preoccupied, I make my exit and close the half door. We watch the boar as it devours first the skins n heids out the pail then while it's head is in the trough scoffing the guts, I nip in for Sanny's pail. Sanny is feeling sick at the sight of the boar having it's lunch and says he is having nothing more to do with pigs, pork, ham or bacon ever again. Winding Sanny up with a story, I tell him, "Do not tell anyone the tale of the boar's lunch."

"Why not?" he says.

"The boar might die with the fur clogging up it's intestines," I say.

Sanny ponders this for a while and offers to go and get loads of water for the boar to drink, to help it's digestion. I tell him this will not work as the water will make the hare fur swell in its gut and make the problem worse. Sanny is turning white with worry so I tell him the only solution would be to get the boar to eat a packet of steel wool or brillo pads.

"Do you think that will work? Because I will go and pinch a packet from the house." Says Sanny.

Beside myself with mirth, I manage to keep a straight face and tell Sanny that the boar is going to be really quite ill, but after eating the brillo pads it might just scrape through. Well!! Sanny is so angry because I had managed to worry him so much about the boar, he picks up one of the pails and starts swinging it at me. Sanny can have a bit of a temper so I make myself scarce.

Looking back down towards the shed I can see Sanny picking up the other pail and going to the house to give Benachie mam them back. She is so pleased not to have to go looking for the pails that, five minutes later he comes out with a piece with raspberry jam. Never ever before did anyone go in and come out with something to eat in between meals. We were so well fed that we did not need to. Sanny halves the piece with me so we are all pals again now and we look forward to our next little adventure.

Sanny and I roam all over the farm, familiarising ourselves with where everything is. We never know when Donal will send us to look for something he needs while in the fields working.

Down in the bottom of the garden Donal has some bee hives which we steer well clear of. He also has a couple of goats tied to a tree on a long rope. The goats are happily munching and chomping away at the grass in the garden. When they see us coming they trot towards us. We stop warily, not sure how long the ropes are. The goats come up to us at the end of their ropes. We make goat and sheep noises at them, mehh, mehh. We do not think they are impressed. Sanny tells them we are all the way up here from Goatbridge, mehh, mehh. and we both laughed uncontrollably at that. The goats looking angry now, charged at us. We thought we knew the length of the ropes so we turned round and stuck our behinds out at them. Wallop, wallop. We are both knocked off our feet. Oh!! That was really sore. We will not be doing that again.

At the far end of the close there is a huge building roughly horseshoe shaped. At one end is the Kert shed which houses the electric generator and a large square tank filled with diesel fuel for the tractors.

Upstairs from this, is the loft, full of corn. A wooden door at the back of the kert shed lets you into the barn where all the hay bales are stored.

A wide wooden ladder goes up to the loft. In the floor of the loft is a six inch hole where some of the corn is slid down a chute to the bruiser. The bruiser machine simply flattens the corn to make it easier for the poultry to digest. The barn is L shaped and there is a large sliding steel door that opens onto the corn yard at the back, giving access for the hay bales to be put in. Another door is an access to the byre where one long wall is separated into stalls with chains hanging in each bay for two cows to be tied up side by side when they are inside. Either for milking or for winter. Above each stall is a large wrought iron basket which can be filled with hay for the cows to eat. The byre has a cobbled floor which can be tricky to walk on. At this time of year with the byre not being cleaned out since winter, there is a foot thick carpet of muck, (straw and cowpat) which we will get started on removing sometime soon. At the other end of the byre is a half door where we can look into the wee byre. This door cannot be opened as the muck on the floor has made it stick.

We go outside, where, in the middle of the U shaped building is the midden, which is a huge steaming pile where all sorts of muck has been dumped. All the muck from the two byres and the henhouse will be dumped out here when we get around to it during our stay.

Our Sanny is starting to look green around the gills again as the smell from the midden starts to take effect.

"Big snokes," I told him,"take big snokes."

Sanny is standing at the edge of the midden taking huge snokes of the midden pong to help him get used to it.

"No, it's not working," He says, still taking huge snokes. Then he sees me and our Senga hanging onto the half byre door, beside ourselves, laughing, while watching him taking huge snokes.

"That's it," he says, as he stormed off. "No way am I ever listening to anything you say anymore."

Who can blame him for that. Still sore with laughing I follow him round the other side of the kert shed.

Then we find it, the wee grey Fergie tractor, sitting at the side of the kert shed. Sanny and I both ran to be first to climb on to the Massey Ferguson tractor which had become an icon of modern agriculture, in those days. Sitting on the driver's seat pretending to drive, Sanny is making tractor noises, dddrrrrrrr, eeehhhh, dddrrrrr, he goes, changing gear while I am sitting on the large mudguard beside him. We cannot wait until hay time to get on the tractor and hook up the kert then go to the hay park to work. Donal also has a large blue Fordson Major tractor that he has loaned to another farmer over the hill at Deuchries. We are going for a walk with him after supper to get the tractor back for hay time. This tractor has a cab mounted on it so cousin Harry, Sanny and I can all get inside with Donal driving.

After supper is all finished we walk over the hill with Donal and we are introduced to the farmer at Deuchries who is a large ruddy faced man with a bunnet similar to Donal that sits on his head at a jaunty angle. Farmer Deuchry, as we call him from now on, is very friendly and tries to negotiate a price for us to go and work for him and bring in his hay.

"Na na, ye winna get them afore I use them to get my hay in first," said Donal.

"Och!! They'll be nae ees efter you're finished wi them then," says farmer Deuchry.

Donal says to him, "Weel weel min, we need to ging hame noo but think on a deal and we can both maybe make some money fae these three fit loons."

They both laughed and shook hands. Donal climbs onto the tractor and we pile in the cab beside him. The tractor roars into life and Donal roars into song.

"There was a wild colonial boy Jack Duggan was his name."

This song is one we will hear many times on the tractor with Donal.

"Belt it out" We say to him.

Donal steers the tractor through the gate and into the field to take us up over the hill back home to Mains of Afforsk.

At the top of the hill we have a wonderful view ahead and we can see the whole farm and beyond. We get a glimpse of "The Pond" shimmering in the evening sunshine, which is nestling just inside the forest at the top edge of Donal's farm.

The pine forest that surrounds most of the farm is in full view and stretches away to the foot of Benachie hill which rises up in the distance. One day soon, we will all be going for a walk up there.

We are all excited and up early for breakfast the next morning as hay making will begin today. Donal is already out in the corn yard fussing about the tractor with the mower attached. A scoot of oil here and a scoot of oil there and everything seems to be ready to go. Donal lines us three boys up and says to me, "OK, Dovit, you are the tallest so you are the mower mannie."

Cousin Harry is not happy about this as he would like to be the mower mannie. Donal knows what cousin Harry is like so he gives him an equally important job.

"Fill up the Fergie with diesel and check the engine oil, that will be your job this morning."

Cousin Harry is chuffed with this task so he goes off with his chest sticking out proudly. Our Sanny says to Donal, "What about me?"

"Weel now," says Donal, "ging in and see mither and ask her for my pipe and baccy and bring it here to me."

Sanny is away running to do this and Donal takes the opportunity to show me what I need to do as a mower mannie. The mower has two iron wheels on an axle with a tractor seat mounted high on top. The blade of the mower, which looks like a long row of shark's teeth, stretches out six feet to the right just in front of the wheels. At the end of the blade is a small wheel which keeps the whole thing from dragging on the ground. Attached to the blade is an iron rod leading to a huge pedal just below and in front of the seat. When the blade is on the ground the pedal is up, when the pedal is depressed the mower blade is lifted up at a 45 degree angle to allow the tractor to turn at the top and bottom of the row. The blade is hooked up like this when the mower is being transported to and from the field. For me to be able to get the blade up I have to slide off the seat and put my whole weight on the pedal. Donal lets me practice a few times so that I know what I need to do when we are in the field.

Donal and I are going to the hay field to start cutting hay after lunch and Sanny and cousin Harry have been found some important work to do for Benachie mam. All the girls have gone out with Aunt Izzie in the car to do some shopping.

I do not need to sit on the mower while we go to the field so I am up in the cab with Donal. With the mower blade up high we have three gates to go through on our way and I have the job of opening and closing these.

Donal has let one of the sheepdogs out to take with us. His name is Glen. Donal says that the dog is really fast and will maybe catch a hare for our dinner. The dog is very friendly and walks beside me when I get off to open the first gate. I tell Donal I will run with the dog to the next gate so carry on without me. The cows in the field are looking at me and Glen trotting in front of the tractor which is not going fast as the path in the field is rough. The cows know the dog but they don't know me, so, cows being nosy by nature come ever closer to me and are trotting along beside us when Glen gives a loud bark to let them know they are too near. The cows quickly run off in another direction and leave us alone. Never having had a pet, I am liking this dog more and more. After the third gate we are now in the hay field. Donal sets the tractor in line for the first cut which will be uphill towards the dry stane dyke at the edge of the forest. While Donal is filling his pipe I notice he has his double barrel shotgun propped up in the tractor beside him so I ask him what he might be able to shoot in the hay field.

"Och!! you never ken, maybe a Roe deer or something else, you jist never ken. Ony wye, let's get started Dovit."

Climbing on to the mower I realise there is nothing to hold onto except the edge of the iron seat. I push the pedal slightly to take the strain off the blade for Donal to unhook it. Slowly I lower the blade to the ground. Donal in the cab now, looks back at me and with a thumbs up we start moving. The iron wheels are turning now and making the blades go side to side, cutting the hay. Donal knows I am now used to the vibration and rumbling of the mower wheels so he speeds the tractor up knowing that the faster the blade goes the better it will cut. We are near the top of the first run so Donal is half round in his seat watching me to see if I am ready to lift the blade on time. Too early and some hay will not be cut, too late and the mower blade will be smashed against the dry stane dyke on the turn. My timing is perfect as we get to the top. Slipping off the seat, I use all of my weight to get the blade up. The tractor makes a tight turn bringing the mower round into line for the next cut. Dropping the blade gently I slip back up onto the seat ready for the downhill run. The tractor is going a little faster so Donal is still sitting half round on his seat to keep an eye on me. Twelve more runs up and down and we are halfway across the park. Five o clock is lowsin time. Donal stops the tractor at the bottom of the park and switches it off. Climbing down off the mower I can hardly walk. My legs are stiff with the strain of keeping me in the seat.

"Where's Glen?" I ask Donal.

Donal lets out a shrill whistle and Glen barks back at him from the top of the park and runs quickly down to stand at his side.

"Okay," says Donal, giving the dog a good clap.

"Lets you me and Dovit ging doon the road for oor teh." He says to the dog.

Leaving the tractor in the park until tomorrow we walk home for oor teh. We do not need to follow the road and can take a shortcut across the parks then across the moss.

The moss is a boggy piece of land that cannot be culti-vated. Over many years it has been used as a dumping ground for redundant equipment, rocks and boulders found when ploughing the rest of the land.

After our supper Donal is having a nap in his big chair so I go out to find my new friend. To my surprise, Glen is waiting for me to come out. Sanny comes over to meet the dog too. Cousin Harry stays well back from Glen. He says it is a crabbit dog, but we suspect he has done something to it in the past. As if to confirm this, Glen growls at him. Sanny and I walk back up to the hay park with Glen.

As soon as we get into the park Glen has his nose to the ground and is on the scent of something in amongst the cut area of the park. Then we see it, halfway up the park is a large hare looking down at us and the dog. The dog is oblivious to this as he is following his nose. Backwards and forwards across the park he runs getting faster and faster as the scent is getting stronger. Then his head goes up as he spies the hare. The hare sees the dog close now and no longer rooted to the spot he goes off like a hare. Glen is now in close pursuit. Swerving to and fro they go, further and further up the park. The hare is up over the dyke and disappearing into the forest so Glen stops. We think he knows a chase in the forest would be pointless. We call Glen down to us but he is already on the scent of some-thing else. Climbing through the dividing fence into the park with cows in it, he is on the trail of another hare. The chase is on again. The nosy cows in the park are starting to run too. This time the hare is too far down the park to make it to the forest so Glen catches it and quickly dispatches it with a shake of his head. Back home we give Benachie mam the hare and she says.

"That's jist grand boys, the butcher will be fine pleased with this one. Fower bob each you get for them."

Over the next few days Glen bags three more hares. We go outside to tell our sisters one night about the chases that Glen has been having.

"We do feel a wee bit sorry for the hares," they said.

Sanny says, "By the way David, I am not feeding that hog again."

Claire, Jinty and Senga are in the barn clearing up, in preparation for the hay bales coming in next week. They show us the den they have made with the two dozen bales that are left over from last year. This is great, there is a tunnel to crawl through that opens into a hidden square space in the middle that we can all fit into. It feels warm in there too. We can hide from cousin Harry here. We ask where cousin Harry is. Claire says, Aunt Izzie, who is Harry's mother, has taken him away home for a few days. Apparently he had been complaining that we were taking over all the good jobs on the farm so Benachie mam had asked Aunt Izzie to take him up the road for a while. We know he will be back in a few days.

Donal and I finished cutting all the rest of the hay park the next day so the mower was brought home and put in a corner of the corn yard. Looking back up at the hay park from the corn yard we can see the straight lines of cut hay. Donal pats me on the back and says to me. "Weel done laddie, you did a grand job up there."

I stand beside him surveying the hay park which is in between two parks. There is the roadside park, full of cows, then to the left, is the tree park, with a tree in the middle and all planted with corn which is still a bit green looking although by the time we are going back to school, the corn will be turning a golden colour and nearly ready for harvesting. Next to that is a park with no name with loads of sheep in it. To the left of that is the hill park, all planted with barley, also a bit green looking. This is the last park on the farm and is up towards Bennachie hill. The parks are in a sort of semi circle at the other side of the moss. They can all be viewed from the farmyard, which is good for Donal to be able to see all the animals without having to walk all the way over the moss.

Tomorrow if the cut hay is dry enough, we will all be going up there to turn it over with a pitchfork so that it can dry on the other side. Hay needs to be dry before it is baled. If it is damp when baled then heat is generated and it can catch fire.

Turning hay in this manner is a really tedious job and cousin Harry soon gets fed up with it and is disappearing over the moss home. Our Sanny is next to go but not before he shows me the blisters on his hands from the wooden handled pitchfork. We all stop and watch the two wee guys trudging home across the moss with their heads down.

All of a sudden their heads go up when they see one of Donals good friends Sandy Ingram of Boghead farm, coming up towards them on his tractor with a strange looking gadget being trailed behind it. The gadget is a huge hay turner. We all turn around to look at Donal who is sitting down on the ground now, filling his pipe and grinning at us. He knew Sandy was maybe coming today, but he was not sure, so he did not tell us. He thought it might be better if we got some hay turning done by hand. Donal knows we would have stuck to the mammoth task but we are all glad that we do not need to turn the whole park by hand, even Donal is happy to sit and have a rest. Sandy Bogie as he is better known, (reference to His farm Boghead) does not hesitate when he gets into the park. With a wave to us and without stopping, he is lined up with the first row and lowering the turner spikes to the ground, off he goes up and down the park at a great rate of knots turning the rows of hay. With nothing for us to do we leave Sandy to do his work and slowly start the trek home.

Then, Donal has a brain wave. Lining us all up he says.

"I will give you a head start and race you all across the moss home."

We say to him, "We will give you a head start."

"Na na ye winna," he says.

"I will coont to ten, then, I will be coming efter yiz."

Donal starts counting.

"Een, twa, three, fower."

We start running as fast as we can across the rough ground. Long reeds growing in the damp ground grab at our legs as we fly past, rocks and boulders too, hidden in the grass, are tripping us up. We are running as fast as we can with our wellies that are two and three sizes too big for us. Well spread out now. Our Claire and Jinty are way in front with their long legs carrying them so fast that us boys and Senga are left lagging behind. Worried about Donal maybe being too old for this run, we look round to see where he is, when, with his bunnet in his hand and pipe firmly clenched in his gums, he flies past us looking like Popeye. With his arms going like pistons, he soon catches the girls and keeps going until he vaults over the last fence and reaches the horse trough in the close.

Donal is sitting on the edge of the trough cupping his hand into the water for a drink. He laughs, as five minutes later we all stagger over beside him for a drink too. What a run that was. Donal has on his heavy tackety boots with turned up toes. We sat looking at him in wonderment. He is in his mid fifties, or maybe older. All his hard work over the years has paid off as he is obviously still a very fit man. We will not be racing him again, any time soon.

As we do not need to work today in the hay park Donal takes us for a run in the car which is an old two tone Vauxhall Cresta with red leather seats. The car is really bouncing up the rough farm road. Donal does not seem to mind that the rough road may be doing damage to the suspension. When we turn on to the main road we find out that the suspension is already well gone. The car seems to float round corners and it is like riding a rollercoaster even though the road is quite smooth.

We are all happy just to be out for a run which ends up at Aunt Izzie's cottage five miles away in the village of Chapel of Garioch.

Cousin Harry is with us and seems pleased to be able to show us where he lives. This cottage is exactly like the Broons from the Sunday Posts But n ben. Aunt Izzie has been baking scones so we have some for our tea. Cousin Harry takes us for a walk round the village. There is a church, a cemetery and a shop which is also the post office. A few houses too. The whole place is surrounded by fields. The only reason I can think of why the village is here is because it is at a junction in the road. Cousin Harry says there are only eight other pupils in his class at the village school. There are thirty pupils in my class at home but Harry doesn't believe me.

Later Donal takes us home just as it is getting dark so he needs to put the headlights on in the car. The bouncing, swaying car points the headlights all over the place. First down to the ground then up to the sky. Absolutely hilarious. We do not think Donal knew what we were laughing at. Safely back to the farm, Benachie Mam has some hot chocolate and some biscuits ready for us before we go up to bed. Donal is already heading out to put the generator off.

Tomorrow we will all be in the hay park working around the baler.

Sandy Bogie is working with us today. Two days after he turned all the hay, it dried very well in the heat of the sunshine we have had. The hay has been stooked into what they call coals that are all over the hay park. Coals are little haystacks about six or seven feet high. The coals are lifted with a pronged attachment on the front of the tractor that lifts them a little off the ground to transport them closer to the baler.

Cousin Harry is driving the little grey Fergie and looking down his nose at us all on the ground. He is bringing the coals down to the baler. The baler is another strange looking machine with a belt going to the power drive pulley on the side of the tractor. When the tractor engine is running, the baler is operating and compacting the hay into bales. The loose hay is lifted up by Sandy bogie with a long handled pitchfork onto a sloping wooden platform that has prongs protruding through it sliding down intermittently. The hay slides down the slope into a hopper that has a nodding donkey like ram, pushing the hay further into the bowels of the machine. Another ram slides the hay horizontally through a long square slide where Donal puts a large horseshoe shaped piece of iron through the hay to the other side and catches the binder twine and pulls it back through and ties the twine in a knot, thus completing a bale.

Depending on how watchful Donal is, he can dictate the size of the bales. Every few minutes a bale comes out at the end and we are waiting to humph it onto one of two flatbed kerts that are parked nearby. Sanny and Senga are lifting one bale between them, I can lift one by myself. Claire and Jinty are up on the kert taking the bales from us and stacking them up towards the front. They get to about five bales high half way down the kert when Donal jumps up to help them get to seven bales high.

Then we all see Aunt Izzie appearing at the bottom of the park with a huge hamper for our lunch. We all stop and sit down for a feast and a well earned rest. We are all thirsty so we dive into the hamper for the water bottles. Donal has a flask of teh and a piece. We have loads of goodies made up by Bennachie mam. An hour later we all thank Aunt Izzie for our lunch and get back to work.

Donal tells cousin Harry to help Claire and Jinty stack the kert as we have enough coals in aboot for noo. He is not pleased at this as he just wanted to sit on the tractor.

"Hi Ho, Hi Ho, it's off to work we go."

We sing to him, without looking at him.

All the hay has been baled now. It took two days of hard work from us all to get this done.

After a week or so working in the park we are all looking very tanned and healthy. Senga being so fair skinned, has got sunburned and is at home with Benachie Mam.

Both kerts have been fully loaded several times now and taken down to the barn to be unloaded. There are no bales left in the park.

While transporting the last of the bales down from the park to the barn, cousin Harry was driving the wee Fergie with the small kert hooked up to it. We were sitting high on top of the bales which were all stacked up but not tied down. Harry aimed the tractor for ruts in the track to rock the kert and hopefully shake us off the top. Once or twice he did this and we all fell off and had to stop and pick up all the bales that had fallen off with us. Harry was laughing, but we did not think it was funny, as we could easily have hurt ourselves. We quickly put the bales back up on the kert. Cousin Harry was grinning at us while we were doing this, knowing full well he was going to try and do it again. Donal saw what Harry was up to, so he stopped his tractor beside us and told Cousin Harry to get off the wee Fergie tractor and let me drive it. I was over the moon.

Oh dear, Harry did not like this at all, so he stood looking like he was in a big huff as I slowly drove past him picking my way past the ruts and trying to go as smoothly as possible. Everyone on top of the loaded kert burst into song as we drove past him.

"Hi ho, Hi ho, it's off to work we go,
We work all day and we get no pay,
Hi ho, Hi ho, Hi ho, Hi ho."

We did not mean to be nasty to cousin Harry. Just as a little lesson for him to learn as we let him walk home.

Later on that evening, after all the bales had been stacked in the barn, we were all in the kitchen for our supper when Harry came in and joined us. We did not mention the incident or make any difference with him, so it was all soon forgotten.

What are we going to do this morning? Benachie Hill says, no work today, as we cannot see it because of the misty rain this morning. Benachie Mam is teaching Claire and Jinty to bake after breakfast so Senga, Sanny and I are sent out to find something to do. Donal left earlier in the car with cousin Harry to (see a man about a dog) apparently.

We go out to the byre and begin to clear it up. A shallow hollow up the middle of the byre which allows the water /pee to run away, is the line we work to first. We scrape the loose dirty straw from the stalls across this line. Then we start at one end with a stall each and dig, scrape, brush and shovel the hard packed straw and cowpats, throwing it all across the shallow ditch. Two hours later, the stalls are all cleared and swept right down to the cobbles. The byre and all the stalls are looking really good.

Being the tallest I agreed to go and get the wooden byre barrow that I saw up against the wall in the corn yard. There is a wide plank of wood from the cobbles outside the byre door up onto the midden. The barrow is heavy enough when empty, when it is full, I struggle to push it up the plank, only managing halfway before it tips to the side and I fall to my knees. The barrow has at least emptied onto the midden. I tell Senga and Sanny not to fill it up so much. We soon get into a method of half filling and emptying the barrow, taking turns running up the plank and heaving the barrow all the way over. By lunchtime we had cleared most of the muck out. We need to move the plank now as the pile in the middle of the midden is getting too steep for us. The byre is looking much better. The midden is really smelling rank with all this freshly disturbed muck. Sanny has given up working again, saying.

"This is really stinking work and is no holiday for me, so, I am doing no more of this slave labour."

Senga and I tell Sanny to take big snokes again but he just stormed off in a rage. We are both in fits, laughing again as he strides away with steam coming out his lugs.

Benachie mam is calling us in for wir denner (our lunch) but Sanny does not hear her as he is round in the corn yard sitting on the big Ford tractor, making big tractor noises. We all troop in and sit at the table, starving as usual. Sanny appeared a little later when his stomach told him it was lunchtime.

After Suppertime that night, Donal walks away over to the park next to the corn yard to bring in the milking cow. We can hear him shouting to the cow. "Weh here, weh here, come awa lass."

The milking cow ambles up the park to the gate and walks past Donal who closes the gate behind her. Bluesy is a massive milking cow that has lived on the farm all it's life. This cow is a sort of shimmery dark blue colour, hence its name. We stand well back to let the cow past us as it comes out of the corn yard. Bluesy is not used to seeing us so she hesitates a little as she comes past, but she knows where to go and is keen to get into the byre to get milked. We do not think Bluesy will be able to get through the narrow door. No problem there, she squeezes her bulk in and turns left up the byre to the stall third from the end. This is her stall. She stands there looking back down the byre at us, then reaching up to the hay we had put up for her earlier, Bluesy starts munching contentedly. Donal brings up the rear and stands gobsmacked at the door when he sees how clean the byre is. Claire, Senga Jinty and I had come back over after lunch and finished the job.

"Weel weel, yiz have been busy the day, whit a grand job yiz have done, am fair prood and pleased, mither will be, ana."

Donal goes into the barn and brings some fresh straw to throw under Bluesy's feet in the stall. The chain is put around her neck to keep her from moving about in the stall just in case she gets startled and kicks or tramples Donal who is kneeling down with a shiny pail placed under the cows udders. With the pail at an angle between his knees, Donal is milking away good style when he points a teat and squirts warm milk at Senga.

"Come awa in aboot and learn how to milk a coo," says Donal.

"Okay," Senga says.

Donal shows her what to do and leaves her to it. It takes her about twenty minutes to milk Bluesy. We can't believe how much milk is in the pail. Standing up, Senga pours some milk into a bowl for the three cats that have been waiting patiently behind us. Donal lets the chain off and Bluesy heads out the byre back to the park. We follow her to make sure she goes. While opening the gate and standing back to let her into the park, Bluesy stops and has a big sniff at us and lets us pat her and rub her head then she carries on back into the park.

It is still dull and raining, so we are all in the kitchen talking to Benachie mam and Donal who is back in his chair smoking his pipe. Donal says

"Abody did a grand job the day mither," he says to Benachie mam.

"Aye, ah heard that, weel done you eens," says Benachie mam.

"What happened to you then?" he asks Sanny.

We wonder how our Sanny is going to answer this, when he goes into his pocket and withdraws a dirty looking stem of a pipe.

"There you go Donal, I found this in the midden for you today."

Sanny hands Donal the stem. On inspection, Donal says, "That's great laddie, I lost this last year when I was cleaning the byre and I really missed it, so, well done."

We cannot believe it when Donal wipes the stem on his jacket, gives it a blow through and swaps it for the stem on his already lit pipe. He lies back in the chair, shuts his eyes and puffs happily away. No matter that the stem had been in the stinking midden for a year. We looked at Benachie mam to see if she was as flabbergasted as we were. No such thing, she never batted an eyelid, she just carried on with some knitting she was doing. Sanny stands grinning at us knowing full well he has exonerated himself, again, the lazy sod.

Life on the farm means we all get involved with what-ever is going on. Aunt Izzie is taking us up to The Pond today to pick Raspberries. The Pond was man made by the forestry commission about twenty years before, so that water would be readily available incase of a forest fire. A long horseshoe shaped wall was built to capture water from two diverted burns that run off Benachie hill. Trees were planted all round the edge of the wall leaving a path to walk around on top of the wall at the water side. The pond is pretty full after the two days of heavy rain we have had since finishing all the work with the hay.

We climb back down the pond wall to where Aunt Izzie is standing with a wicker basket handing out syrup cans with a string on them, for us to put the raspberries in. We look around ourselves and see we are in a huge patch of wild juicy raspberries. Picking raspberries is quite painful with the small thorns on the raspberry bushes ripping the backs of our hands. We soon get used to the thorns. This raspberry patch proves to be very productive. When our cans are full we go to Aunt Izzies basket and empty the contents in. Aunt Izzie has one of the milking pails on the crook of her arm and after an hour of picking it is half full. The basket she left for us is nowhere near half full and that is with four of us tipping all of our cans into it.

"Maybe you are all eating more than you are putting in the tin."

Says Aunt Izzie with a smile. We carry on picking until lunch time. The basket is almost full and Aunt Izzies pail is nearly overflowing. She tells us we do not need to come back after lunch as we have got plenty of rasps now for Benachie mam to make jam with. Struggling into the kitchen we put the heavy load of rasps on to the table, where Bennachie mam inspected them. She has looked them over now and with a big grin she says.

"Well done, the baker mannie was in aboot the day so here you go." Handing us all a big sticky bun each to eat after our lunch.

While we eat our lunch, Benachie mam gets a massive pot half filled with water onto the range to boil. Aunt Izzie is pouring the rasps into a basin of cold water to rinse them. When the pot of water is boiling the raspberries are added, making the pot nearly full. An awful lot of sugar goes in too, then the pot is stirred slowly for a while and left to simmer. The smell is amazing, we cannot wait to get some later with our sago pudding. Claire and Jinty got out the jam jars from under the stairs and began washing and drying them ready for the jam to be poured in. Aunt Izzie chased us outside to play as we were now getting in the way of jam production.

Sitting in a row along the edge of the horse trough, Sanny, Senga, cousin Harry and myself are eating our sticky buns when we notice we have an audience of hens and ducks looking hungrily at our buns. Breaking small pieces off, we throw them some, but not much, as the buns are too good to waste on just any old chickens. Anyway, we had fed them all before we went to the pond earlier, greedy sods.

Claire and Jinty have been relieved of Jam duties for the time being so we ask them to take us back up to the pond.

"OK, let's go then," said Claire.

We walk back up to the pond, past the raspberry patch that still has loads of raspberries in it. We climb the pond wall and peep quietly through the trees to see five or six wild ducks swimming and floating on the water. Quite suddenly one of them dives down and we look to see where it will pop back up. Some of them are diving down looking for food and generally going about their business in the reeds and margins. Watching the ducks for five minutes is too long for Sanny and cousin Harry. Bored, they jump up and start making a noise. The ducks also make a noise as they take off from the water and fly away over to the far side and land there, quickly swimming into the long reeds where we can no longer see them. They are probably nesting there. We start to walk round the pond as far as we can go until we are running out of wall. The water here is shallow and very weedy but we know it would still be too deep for us to wade through. We turn around to walk back the way we came when we notice that the water is now flat calm after the ducks' cacophony earlier. There are little ever increasing rings appearing all over the pond. Brown trout are rising to sip small flies and pond skaters hatching on the surface. We sat down again to watch. The water is really clear and we can actually see some trout, oblivious to us, swimming past, as they search for emerging nymphs and flies. This is a great place to sit and watch all sorts of wildlife. Trout, ducks, and even buzzards wheeling high overhead as they float in the thermals, calling to each other. Donal is pleased to know there are some ducks on the pond when we tell him later.

"I will need to get my gun and go up there some o these nichts and shoot oor supper."

Sitting quietly at breakfast one morning we can hear a really loud bellowing and mooing noise, coming down from the direction of the roadside park.

We say,

"Oh my!! Something must be wrong." It was so loud.

"Na na noo,"Says Donal,

"It's just Sandy Bogie bringing a puckle o his nout for Charlie the Bull."

The bull recognises the float and knows that Sandy has cows in there for him. As Sandy bogie slowly makes his way in aboot, the bull follows him, bellowing and crashing his way through a fence and into the moss. Sandy parks up and quickly lets the cows into the moss to calm the bull down before he does any more damage.

Sandy and Donal are standing about newsing, so we go about our business of the morning, feeding the hens and ducks. We feed the big boar too. He easily survived the episode of the hare skins and heids, without the help of the brillo pads.

The four cows are left in the moss with the bull for a few days, then, Sandy bogie brings his float to take them home again to Boghead, hoping to have some calves sometime soon.

"Oh, I wish I was where the Gadie rins, the Gadie rins,
the Gadie rins,
Oh I wish I was where the Gadie rins,
At the Back o Benachie."

Our mam used to sing this song to us and today, Donal is taking us for a walk up to the top of Benachie hill, where, among other things, we will be able to see where the Gadie burn rins.

We are outside the porch pulling long thick socks on before putting our wellies on. Donal points to his boots with the turned up toes and tells us, "These are the boys for uphill walking."

A crook in his hand, Donal sets off. Picking up a long stick each, we follow him up past the right hand side of the pond and along the bottom of the hill park full of sheep. We work our way into the forest listening to Donal telling us of his exploits when he worked with the forestry commission, planting and harvesting trees.

No tractors in those days. Donal started work at four-teen years of age using a large Clydesdale horse for dragging logs to the forest road, where they would be loaded onto long trailers and trucks to be transported to sawmills all over the Country. Donal bought his own Clydesdale horse after a year working with the forestry commission.

When there was no forestry work Donal and his horse travelled all over Aberdeenshire, working for farmers bringing in their hay or harvest. In a few years, Donal had earned himself a good reputation of being dependable and hardworking.

Recently married to Benachie Mam he heard that a hill farm called Mains of Afforsk had become available for lease from the government. He made enquiries and subsequently leased the farm for ten years. After three or four hard years into the lease someone from the government approached him and offered to sell him the property. The princely sum of £2000 was agreed and that is how Donal now owned the farm.

We are climbing out of the forest and up Bennachie which is mainly rocky ground covered with heather. Thirsty in the summer heat now, Donal shows us how to get a drink. With his hand to his ear and listening carefully, he walks over to a large clump of heather and pulling it back exposes a small pool of clear water fed from a spring coming down the hill. He cups his hand and drinks from the sparkling clear water. We follow suit and after a five minute rest we are eager to get to the top. We don't think Donal heard the trickling water as we know he is deaf with the noise of the tractors. We think he knew the water pool was there.

Nearing the top Donal stops and tells us about Esson's croft, the outline of which we can see below us on the East side of the hill. This croft was made by a man called Esson who moved onto the hill with his family in the late 1800's.

He cultivated an area of land that apparently did not belong to anyone. For twenty five or thirty years the Esson family were living on Benachie, then disappeared as mysteriously as they had come. The overgrown outline of the croft and the ruined steading can still be seen from a distance to this day.

We are nearly at the top. The last part is hard going as it is all sharp, broken, vitreous rocks that have come from the vitreous fort that had been on the top of the hill at one time in past history. The collapsed fort is what makes Bennachie look like a volcano to us from a distance.

The Mither Tap is the actual name of this area. Standing up there we are in awe looking at the patchwork map of Aberdeenshire, spreading out before us. The view all around is amazing.

Looking South back the way we had come is the pond shimmering in the sun. Just beyond that is the farm we have just walked from. We look East, twenty miles to the City of Aberdeen and beyond to the North Sea, which is only just visible on the horizon. Looking North to the "Back o Bennachie." We can see half way down the hill, there is a car park, then an easy path to the top. Why did we not come up this way? We can see several quarries in the distance where a lot of the granite for building the granite city comes from. The Gadie burn is away in the distance too. Donal points out Sandy Bogie's farm and Aunt Izzie's cottage, which is appropriately called Benachie Cottage in the small village of Chapel of Garioch.

All too soon we start the long trek home. Going downhill would be much easier, or so we thought. No chance, the heather was tugging at our legs as we tried to stride through it. Falling sometimes over rocks and tripping in the heather we learned to follow Donal as he picked his way down without mishap. Donal the hill farmer triumphs again with his superior knowledge. He is well versed in travelling up and down these hills even in the dark, looking for lost sheep, or more likely, stalking and hunting the Laird of Pittodrie's deer.

Benachie mam is waiting for us with the tea ready, listening to our stories of the day. She said she could see us on top of the hill then making our way down, and that is how she knew when to put the tea on. After tea we all go out to see if we can see anyone on the hill. No, we can see no one. Great eyesight our Benachie mam. Maybe nearly as good as Donal's lugs, we thought.

There is great excitement today. Aunt Polly is coming to visit the farm so we have to scrub ourselves clean. Except Sanny. Aunt Izzie sits a basin of warm water outside on a stool in the garden for us to wash in. Topped up with some hot water from the kettle, we take turns dipping our heads in and using soap to work up a lather to wash our hair, faces, hands and neck. Even the wellies have been washed. Sanny does not remember Aunt Polly and does not see what all the fuss is about, so he hides when the garden wash time is happening.

Aunt Polly, dressed in a very smart light blue ladies suit steps out of the car along with our Aunt Dorothy, who is dressed in a Royal blue ladies suit and looking very posh indeed with her feather in her hat. They arrive in a car driven by Uncle Max, who has only one arm.

The empty right sleeve of Uncle Max's sports jacket is tucked into his pocket. We are all standing in a row along the garden wall, to be greeted by the Aunties and Uncle. They all do the hugging and head patting thing and naming all our names.

"How do they know who we all are?" Asked our Senga.

"Because they are our mam's relations." Says Claire.

Everyone troops into the kitchen to see Benachie mam and Donal, who is in his usual chair. Loud chatter starts up between all the adults who are talking about people and stuff we know nothing of, so, one by one we quietly sneak back outside to play and leave them in peace to talk and have their tea. A few minutes later Uncle Max comes out of the porch and lights a cigarette. He is dressed in a smart checkered sports jacket and wearing a yellow cravat. Us younger ones only vaguely remember him so he asks Claire about our mam and wee eck, (the oul man.)

"Is your dad still working in the Iron work?" He asks.

"Yes" I say.

I proceed to tell him of my exploits at the oul man's work.

We can see that our Sanny is beside himself with questions for Uncle Max and his one arm. We try to keep Sanny at bay but as soon as there is a little lull in the conversation he jumps in with the burning question.

"Where is your other arm then, Uncle Max?"

Uncle Max, pretending to be shocked at the question, looks at us all one by one and bending down to Sanny he says into his lug,

"Hitler's got the blasted thing, so he has. I was shot down over Germany in my bomber during the war and taken prisoner by Hitler himself. My arm was ripped off in the crash and he kept it."

We are all amazed at this as we did not know we had a war hero in the family. Donal comes outside and hearing the tail end of Uncle Max's story, smilingly lights his pipe up. We are all agog at Uncle Max and his stories but Sanny is not finished with all of his questions yet.

"How do you manage to drive with only one arm?"

Uncle Max piles us all into his car and proceeds to drive us backwards and forwards up and down the cobbled close like a maniac. Our brains are rattling at the end of his demonstration. When changing gear with his left arm he simply leans onto the steering wheel with his chest to keep the car steady. He only had to show proficiency at doing this to the authorities so they would let him continue to drive after the war. Donal is still watching and listening to all of this with much amusement.

Little did we know that Uncle Max had lost his arm in a conveyor belt accident in a fish processing factory in Aberdeen, before the war, so he never got to bomb Hitler either.

Later in the day Aunt Polly nabbed Sanny when he passed by her.

"What is this then Sanny?" she said.

Pulling down his collar and looking at his black neck.

"This is not good enough, is it?"

She promptly marched Sanny out to the porch sink, bent him over and proceeded to wash his neck in cold water with the cloth that was lying there. She scrubbed and scrubbed really hard to get Sanny's neck clean, then realising that she was trying to scrub off his tan line, she turned him round and washed his face clean. Sanny, rubbing his sore neck, came back into the kitchen where we all laughed at him for dodging the earlier warm wash he could have had. We knew that Aunt Polly was a stickler for cleanliness, that is why we had conformed earlier.

Over the course of the eight weeks we were at the farm, we met a lot of different people. Visitors for Benachie mam, visitors for Donal, or visitors for them both. At times, we were also taken out to visit other farmers and their wives. We would be all scrubbed up again and maybe not even get out of the car on some of these visits.

Aunt Izzies husband, our Uncle Jim, who was a short chubby Irishman, came one day to do some jobs in the house. He had a very thick Southern Ireland accent coupled with some of the North East Scotland Doric he had picked up in the few years he had lived in this area. Listening to him talking sometimes, we struggled to understand what he was saying, so we stayed out of his way and let him get on with his work. Donal came back from wherever he had been and spoke to Uncle Jim about some of the work he needed him to do. Turns out, Uncle Jim would be needing us to work with him at another farm tomorrow.

Uncle Jim arrived the next morning in his car to pick us up. While he was inside talking to Benachie mam we all piled into his car. When he came out and saw us in the car he laughed and said.

"Na na noo, the car is staying here, so oot ye all git."

"What's happ'nin then?" we asked him.

"Well, we need the big tractor and the big kert, so let's go and get them."

We follow him to the corn yard where the tractor and the kert are standing waiting on us. Donal must have cleeked them up earlier. Four of us sitting on the kert and two of us in the cab with Uncle Jim. Off we went up the road. Sitting on the kert is horrendous. Uncle Jim is singing and belting out Irish ditties at the top of his voice.

"There was a wild colonial boy, Jack Duggan was his name,"

"Oh Paddy Mcginty's goat."

All the while, driving up the farm road like a madman. We are bouncing all over the place, feeling every bump and pothole in the road. Uncle Jim does not hesitate at the top and turns left onto the main road. This is much better. The tar road is smooth so Uncle Jim puts the tractor into high gear and thumps down the road as fast as he can go. (Probably about 28 mph) Feels a lot faster though, when sitting on the kert. After a mile or so we turn right into another farm road. Going along this more level tree lined road is OK now, as we are now used to the rumbling we are getting on the kert. We arrive at Humphry's farm.

The Humphry family are abroad on holiday and we are doing them a favour picking up and taking away some tree stumps from a field. About two hundred trees in the area we have now stopped at, were cut down the year before, then sold to the saw mill. The stumps were all pulled out of the ground by a huge bulldozer and left to dry. Our job is to load the stumps onto the kert and take them away. When the area is cleared it will be ploughed and some sort of crop planted in it. Some of the stumps are so heavy we cannot lift them so we leave them for Uncle Jim. Two hours later the kert is full so we climb up on top and hold on for dear life. Uncle Jim takes his time going home as he does not want to lose his load.

We are all so weary and hungry we fall in the kitchen door looking for something to eat and drink. Uncle Jim hooks a hydraulic hose from the kert to the tractor and tips all the stumps off behind the hen hoose at Donal's little sawmill. He pops his head round the kitchen door and says to us,

"Same time tomorrow then."

Laughing, he leaves to go home. Benachie mam knows how to cheer us up though. She has been baking all day so there are loads of different cakes on the go.

As with any other work we took on at the farm, we did go back the next day and finished clearing all the dreaded stumps at Humphries farm.

Alas, alas, alas. The time has nearly arrived for us to go back home to Coatbridge. Eight weeks have passed so quickly. We have all adapted to the farm routines, so we do not want to think about returning home.

First though, Sanny and I had to go for a walk over to Jimmy Shand's farm for a back to school haircut.

The walk is about three miles as Jimmy Shand's farm is a bit further on past Humphry's farm. To pass the time on our walk we count the flattened puddocks (frogs) on the road. So many we lose count.

Jimmy is a really old farmer who had learned to cut hair in the army in the first World war. His one and only style is a bowl cut. Jimmy, with his big red shiny face, is waiting in his kert shed to do the haircuts. Sanny and I take it in turn to sit on a three legged stool to have our hair shorn. We cannot believe the amount of hair he cuts off. Eight weeks since we had our crew cut and our hair has now grown over our lugs.

(This seriously bad haircut would need to be rectified as soon as possible at Mclays the barber.)

Our Senga is with us as always and is still laughing at the bowl cuts when we are invited into the Shand's farmhouse for our tea. We washed our hands at the outside tap before going into the huge warm welcoming kitchen.

Jimmy Shand was already sitting smoking his pipe in a similar wing back chair to Donal's. He was almost lying on his back on the chair with his backside hanging off the front edge looking at us over the top of his huge stomach. The Shand's are really nice people and Mrs Shand is also a great baker and cook. We are well looked after and are reluctant to leave. Jimmy Shand offers us a lift home and we say our thanks and goodbyes to Mrs Shand. Outside we see no car, only a grey Fergie tractor with a cab on it. Jimmy says, "Nae need for expensive cars, this tractor does me just fine."

To my knowledge, Jimmy never ever owned a car but relied only on his Fergie to get him about. We three pile in and Jimmy takes us slowly home. On the journey Jimmy tells us about him and Donal going to the market in Inverurie at a time before there were any cars or tractors on the road. A horse and kert is what they travelled to market in. Both of them roaring drunk after a good day trading at the market they set off home lying on the back of the kert, knowing full well the horse knew how to get them up the road and home safely.

Our last night was spent talking about the great times we have had and the sights we have seen. Some of the unfinished tasks we still have to do will not let us stay any longer.

After breakfast we are all ready and waiting for Aunt Izzie to take us to the station. Dressed in our best once again, Senga, Sanny and I go outside for a last look around at everything. Glen is waiting for me outside but when I go to give him a friendly pat he growls at me. Donal comes round the corner and puts Glen in the kennel.

"He disna' recognise you all clean and dressed up," says Donal.

I am disappointed at this and it only adds to the sadness of us going home.

Aunt Izzie is ready for us to go so we all say our good-byes to Benachie mam and Donal.

"The place will not be the same without you eens," they said.

After more hugs and pats on the head, I think Benachie mam had a wee tear in her eye as we piled into the car then Aunt Izzie reversed along the close and turned up towards the main road. At the heid of the road we stop and look back to see Benachie mam waving a white dish towel in the distance. Turning onto the main road to Aberdeen Aunt Izzie says. "Weel weel an, that's the holiday a ower."

Our heads go down in the back of the car. Not a word was spoken all the way to the station. The train journey home was not much better. We remember very little of the journey. The fiddle de dee of the train on the tracks has really faded now. Sanny does not even look at the emergency brake chain.

Back home, it is really great to see Mam and all the rest of the family. Really exhausted and tired that night we just wanted to fall into bed. Mam is looking at our bowl cuts and she says, "Oh michty me, you two boys will need to go for another crew cut the morn'."

"Oh good, we can't wait for that," we say.

Going into bed that night we can hear Senga telling the rest of the girls in the other room about Jimmy Shand and his haircuts.

"No laughing at us yous," I said. Anyway, they still all burst out laughing.

Chapter 13

We join the Lifeboys.

Oh when the saints, oh when the Saints
Go marching in.

Back to school after the exciting and busy days at the farm we slowly settle down to a normal routine. School is out, so I jump over the wall to go down the sannyhole and home.

What a shock I get. Bulldozers have been taking away a lot of the sannyhole towards the iron works. I stand and look over a cliff edge at the new road below me. Massive dump trucks are running round this huge oval shaped road with large piles of different colours of ore in the middle. There is a conveyor belt stretching from one end to the other with a boom stacker at one end. The dump trucks are being loaded with ore by a huge wheel shovel, then they tip into a sunken hopper for the conveyor belt to carry the ore away. This is a disaster. I need to find Tam and find out what is happening. Tam tells me that the machines had been working for two months now but they are finished so we still have half the sannyhole to play in. Great, I thought. Tam told me to meet him after my tea and he would show me something. After tea I meet up with Tam and we go over the sannyhole to the cliff edge and he points to the top, near the school wall where I can see that some of the cliff has collapsed creating a long slope of sand all the way down to the new road. Tam runs up to the top and takes a header down the hill creating an avalanche of sand behind him. That looks superb, so I do the same and tumble head-long down the slope. At the bottom we shake off the sand and start the climb back up. After half an hour of this, we are totally exhausted and end up sitting on the top of the cliff surveying our lost play area and our newly created one.

"At least we still have some trees left for the next couple of years bonfires." says Tam.

Tonight, Sanny and I are going along to the Baptist Church hall in Corsewall Street to join the Lifeboys. Cousin George from Langloan is there too. We have a great time, with various activities going on over the evening. The best thing tonight is the fact we were each given our badges and caps to take home. Mam knows a shop for us to go and get the jumper for the rest of our uniform. There are three groups in the life boys named after missionaries in Africa. Sanny and I are in the Livingston group. So called, after David Livingstone the great explorer and missionary from Blantyre. We are given a task every week of collecting silver paper or used stamps for charity. How this is a help for charity we do not know but the fact we make the effort every week gets us points on the little race track with a car representing each group on it. The more you collect, the farther along the track your car goes. There is a prize at the end of the year for the winning group.

At school, I sometimes help the Jannie, who is a friend of the oul man's. Once a month a huge truck arrives with a load of coke for the school boilers. It takes the Jannie two days to shovel this down the chute into the boiler house.

My pal Bob and I help him now and again to shovel the coke down the chute.

During one of my visits to the boiler house I noticed three or four very large string bags full of silver milk bottle tops. These have been collected over a long period of time from all the little bottles of milk we get every morning. I asked the Jannie if I could have one.

"Of course you can, son, help yourself."

This is great news, I cannot wait to take them to the Lifeboys. When it comes to the part of the night where we take our saved silver paper to the leader at the front of the hall I proudly walk out with the string bag of milk bottle tops. The bag is nearly as tall as I am. The leader is amazed at this. He is at a loss for words and he does not know how far to move the car on the track either. Finally, moving the car towards the front, away ahead of the other two teams he thanked me for my efforts and ingenuity. The other Livingston team members are over the moon too. Next week I have an even bigger bag of bottle tops. The leader sees me arriving with them, so, before I can take the bag into the hall he asks me to put the bag in the boot of his car. Quietly he says to me that he is very impressed with my efforts, but, would I mind not bringing any more as the other groups are so far behind us on the track that they may have given up. Also, the smell from the sour milk tops was unbearable in his house when he took them home last week. I hadn't thought of that. The leader wanted to know where they had come from. After telling him the story of the Jannie and the coke we shovelled, he hoped I would still help the Jannie. I had no problem with that.

"You are a good boy and we are glad to have you here," he said.

Great, my career as a Lifeboy had started brilliantly, then fallen away drastically. That's what I thought for a wee while anyway.

Sanny and I kept up going to the Lifeboys group for one or two years. We had learned to march there so we marched everywhere, especially if we had our tacketty boots on. We polished the large brass badge with brasso before going along to the meetings with our hats on. Every Monday, Sanny, with his hat at a jaunty angle and me with mine sitting on straight, we would take the boredom out of the walk and march all the way down Corsewall Street. Saluting each other and giving each other marching orders all the way.

"By the left, quick march, eft, eft, eft ight eft. By the right, riiiight wheel" and into the Church hall.

There is great excitement today in the family. Uncle Johnny's coming home after three years working in Thailand. Not only that, he is bringing his wife with him. We have a new Auntie and we are all excited to meet her.

Uncle Johnny and Aunt Songsri have been home and rested for a week now so we can all go and visit them. We all troop into Wee Granny's house to see a vision sitting on Granny's couch. A beautiful looking lady smiling at us all. Aunt Songsri wanted to know all our names and ages, and how we were doing at school.

Uncle Johnny had already left for the pub to meet his brother, the Oul man.

We were all amazed at the time that Aunt Songsri took to talk to each one of us individually before we left for home. She even remembered all our names as we trooped out. Songsri and our Mam would quickly become very good friends. We used to run up the street to meet her when we knew she was coming to visit. Songsri always seemed to have a presence when in a room and was such a calming influence when she entered and oh boy, what a cook she was.

Chapter 14

Away day.

Glory Glory Hallelujah

This morning as usual, I got up early for school and out the door, still eating my breakfast. School is the furthest thing from my mind, for today, I am bunking off for the very first time along with my classmate Bob.

A few weeks ago on a Sunday, the oul man had taken the family on a trip to Glasgow. Not just Glasgow in particular but to The Maclellan Art Gallery. An hour on the blue train and we were at Queen St Station. From there we walked to the Art gallery which took the best part of an hour.

On the way, we saw many sights, trolley buses, trams and some men on horses and kerts. The streets of Glasgow were really busy with lots of people going here, there and everywhere.

Entrance into the art gallery is free. Inside, there are many wonders and exhibits from all over the world. We wander all over the place looking in awe at dinosaur bones, fossils, stuffed tigers and lions. Spears along with bows and arrows. What a wondrous place. We have never seen anything like it. We spent many hours there that day.

On the way back we had a trip on the tiny underground train that has a circular route all around and below the city. The speed of the train going through the tunnels is frightening and we are all glad to get off back at Queen Street. On the blue train home I remember sitting quietly, thinking, we have been kept in a bubble while all this city life is going on all around us and not very far from where we live. I make a mental note to myself to explore my surroundings more often.

Hence, the planned trip with Bob. When telling Bob about the art gallery I could see his eyes light up and he suggested dogging the school to go there next week. The blue train, this time, is a whole lot busier. People going to and from work. We get some strange looks from the ticket collector who asks us why we are not at school. Quick as a flash, Bob says, "We are going on a field trip to the Art gallery as part of a school project."

The ticket collector seemed to accept this explanation.

We go on the underground and get off at Kelvingrove, which is the station near the art gallery. Like my sisters and brothers were, Bob is amazed at the exhibits in the art gallery. We even go upstairs to the actual art paintings on show there. We sit on a bench seat admiring the huge paintings that go from floor to ceiling. We learn about Charles Rennie Macintosh, the Glasgow designer from the 1800s. We are not impressed with his furniture.

While trying out some of the high backed Macintosh chairs one of the uniformed caretakers overheard us commenting on how uncomfortable a particular chair was and told us to leave immediately.

"Do not just go downstairs, go all the way out of the building," he said.

Alas, our tour of the art gallery is over for now. It was nearly time for us to go anyway.

Back on the underground to Queen Street station and the blue train we go. "What if we get found out dogging the school?" I say.

"We will think of something," says Bob.

I cannot remember if we got into trouble or not, but we never did it again.

My life at home was too much fun for me to be getting into trouble with dogging school or any other silly exploits.

In a large family in the mornings, there is always something going on. Someone is always having a crisis, somebody can't find their pencils for school, somebody stole my shoe laces.

"Mam!! I have a sore stomach, I can't go to school today and I can't find my homework anyway."

My plan was to always be up and away before all this hoohah started.

One morning though, I was glad to be just a little late.

A mad howling was heard coming from the living room one winter morning. Sanny and I could not work out who the howler was, only that it was one of my sisters. We braved it out and quietly sneaked into the living room to see what the problem was. Our Claire was standing in her stocking soles on the carpet with her brand new boots in her hand with no heels on them. The heels were sitting on the hearth in front of the fire. Jinty had gone out earlier to do a paper round with her pal. As it was winter and deep snow on the ground she decided to borrow Claire's boots knowing she would be back before Claire left for work.

While Jinty was out walking in the snow the dampness and wetness had penetrated the supposed leather and separated the heel from one of the boots. Jinty picked up the heel and put it in her pocket. A few hundred yards further on and the second heel parted from the other boot. Jinty picked it up and finished her paper round doing a funny walk home with the soles of the heel-less boots at an angle. Jinty sat the heels in front of the fire with the boots carefully on top to dry. Claire came into the living room to look for her boots as they were not where she left them. Seeing them in front of the fire she lifted the boots, leaving the heels behind and that's when the howling started. Sanny and I were howling now too, with laughter. We promptly left for school just in case any blame might be flung in our direction.

Chapter 15

I have a job.

The lord is my Shepherd I shall not want.

Today I have a Saturday job. Ted Fagan, who jointly owns a piggery with his brother behind the Bellshill Maternity Hospital also sells firewood. Ted stopped in his lorry one day and asked me if I wanted a job delivering firewood. I asked him how much the pay would be.

"Four Bob plus tips. The quicker the firewood goes, the quicker you get home."

This sounded OK to me, so I told him I would give it a go.

Saturday morning, I am waiting at the top of the Avenue when I see a green and red lorry coming round the Gartsherrie roundabout loaded with firewood. Ted's nephew Jimmy is in the lorry and he jumped out to let me in. Jimmy climbed on the back and we set off to the first customer.

Ted comes out of the lorry with me. Jimmy has a sack of wood ready for us to take to the customer. The firewood is actual railway sleepers cut into squares on a small sawmill at the piggery. The smell of preservative creosote is quite overpowering from the wood. Lifting my first bag onto my shoulders I can feel the clogs as they are called, digging into my back.

"Half a crown a bag son, you will soon get used to it." Says Ted.

While I am emptying the bag into the customers bunker I can hear Ted and Jimmy shouting at the top of their voices, Fiiieeeeerrrrwooood. Back out to the lorry, Jimmy has three more bags filled up for me. Over the course of the day Jimmy fills the bags at each stop and I humph them into the customers. Ted sits in the cab giving orders and shouting out the window "Fiieeeerrrwoooood."

The run takes us all over Townhead, Gartsherrie and Sunnyside. Sometimes Ted sends me up a close to give a shout out to potential customers. Standing at peoples' back doors I say very quietly to myself "Fiiiiieeeeerrrrw- wooooood, Fiiiiieeeeeeerrrrwoooooood."

Then repeat quietly, several times. Back at the Lorry, Ted and Jimmy are still shouting.

"I didn't hear you shouting much Davie."

"It would be hard for you to hear me over yours and Jimmy's voices." I told him.

The lorry is empty at last and Ted is dropping me back at the top of the Avenue.

"Do you know anyone to help Jimmy on the back of the lorry? " He asks. "Our Sanny can come with me next week," I told him. With a big thumbs up, Ted drives back over the Gartsherrie roundabout with a black cloud coming out the exhaust of his old Bedford four wheel tipper lorry.

Into the house and up the stairs, I sit and count the money I had earned for a day's hard graft. Four bob from Ted and six bob in tips. This time Mam gets the tips and I get the four bob.

The following week Sanny comes along with me and helps Jimmy on the back of the lorry. Sanny gets two bob for his efforts and he is quite happy with that.

Some of the sleepers are sodden and this makes some of the bags really heavy. One or two Saturdays on the fire-wood when it is winter and raining are really hard to put up with. Ted is a good laugh to work with but the job is really tough going. Sanny and Jimmy are on the back of the lorry, exposed to the elements all the time. What a filthy state we are in sometimes when we get home. Sanny and I resolve to get another job for ourselves.

As luck would have it, a few days later, I meet Nichol the tattie and egg man, who is the owner of Waverley Brand Potatoes, to be exact. Unknown to me, Nichol delivered a tray of two and a half dozen eggs and a 56lb bag of pota-toes to my mother at our house every week.

"Hello son, I hear you are looking for a job?"

"Yes" I say. "When can I start?"

"Right now if you like."

I tell mam about the job but she already knew as she had spoken to Nichol about me. Out I go into Nichol's van and away to the next chapter.

Chapter 16

I have a better job

Oh happy day.

Two weeks off school and my first day out on the van with Nichol, selling potatoes and eggs. We need to load the van up at the depot first. There are 30 dozen eggs in a wooden box in the back of the van. We stacked pre-packed 14lb bags and 7lb bags of potatoes in rows in the van too.

Ready for action now, Nichol drives us to Baillieston, which is a large housing estate in the East side of Glasgow. I am worried about what I need to shout to sell tatties and eggs, so I asked Nichol and he replied.

"No need to shout here son, we are delivering to existing customers."

This is great news.

Carrying two 14lb bags in each hand and a box of eggs under each arm we start delivering our goods. Getting to a customer's door, we knock and see if anyone is in, if not, we leave the potatoes and eggs on the step and the money will be collected either on Friday night by the collector, or next week when we deliver again. On to the next customer to do the same.

This arrangement works very well for Nichol and saves us carrying heavy bags back to the van. I absolutely love this job. Going home much cleaner after a day's work is good too.

There is a different run every day, Baillieston, Carntyne, Easterhouse, Barlanark, Buddhill, Maryhill and Shettleston. Some of the East Glasgow housing estates are reputed to be troublesome but I have never met nicer or kinder people anywhere.

The first five days go quickly and I have learned the runs quite well. Nichol keeps firing questions at me about where we have been. This is a bit like, The knowledge, for taxi drivers.

Friday night and we are going back into Barlanark to do more of the same. When we finish the Friday afternoon run, Nichol takes me to the depot to load up again, then, to his mother inlaw's house for dinner. One slap up meal later and with Angus on board, (Nichol's father in law) we go into Barlanark. Barlanark has streets and streets of blocks of three storey high flats, this is where we go.

Running up and down the stairs is no problem for me as I am very fit. On a Friday night most people are at home so there are no delays with deliveries. Nichol gives me a cash float so that I can give people change if necessary, to save me going up and down to the van. This has been a long day and I am really tired now. Nichol says to me.

"Don't worry son, Saturday is only a half day."

Yippee from me.

Saturday, and we are in Carntyne. Nichol stops as we turn into the top of the housing estate and picks up two boys the same age as me. We introduce ourselves. One is called John, the other is Kenny. These guys are very loud and full of fun. They tell me that Glasgow people are known to be wide, but they are better than that, they are double wide. "OK." I say to myself, you guys are worth watching then. First stop and we are all at the back of the van getting our instructions. John and Kenny disappear quickly, loaded down with as much as they can carry. Nichol points to a few customers' houses for me to go to. We soon get through all the customers in the area with John, Kenny and I running our legs off. We have sold as much this Saturday morning as we have done on any full day during the week. Nichol is delighted. At the end of the run the two boys are waiting on their pay. Nichol hands the money over they are due and away they go delighted. Nichol asks me if I had noticed anything wrong this morning. "Absolutely I did. Those boys are charging customers a shilling more than we are for a 14lb bag of potatoes."

"Spot on." Says Nichol.

"I have been watching them too, so that is why they got £1 each for their efforts this morning and you are getting £3. They are not stealing from me but they are overcharging the customers who will talk to each other at some point and then they will be found out in their little scam."

Brilliant, I thought, the £3 will be on top of the money I earned all the rest of the week. The week had been really busy and had gone quickly, even though it has been hard work I have learned a lot and I am delighted with my pay of £9 plus tips. My tips came to £4. So in total on Saturday afternoon I had £13. Handing mam £10 was a good feeling. She tried to give me back £2 saying I had worked really hard, so I deserved more. I refused and told her that I knew she needed it so keep it and if she needed more just to ask me. Under Sanny's bed I kept a shortbread tin with all my money in it. My earnings for this week have been added, less £1 for goodies later. The total in the tin is unknown to me as I want a surprise at the end of the two week holiday.

On Saturday night when the ice cream van comes I go with Sanny to buy a large bowl of ice cream, Irn Bru and sweeties.

Back in the house, mam has cups and glasses out on the table. We all line up for a big dollop of ice cream and a splash of Irn Bru each. Mam sits in the living room with us as we wait for the Saturday night movie starting. Clack clack clacking of teaspoons mixing up the ice cream and Irn Bru is quite loud. I hope we are all finished by the time the movie comes on.

Cups and glasses collected and washed. We sit down to watch the film, with the sweets I had bought in a bowl on the table for everyone to help themselves. Mojos, penny whoppers, lucky tatties, lucky bags, rainbow drops, love hearts and penny caramels were the choices we had.

The black and white film is great but it is almost finished as the sweets in the bowl begin to dwindle.

(In the film, James Stewart is sitting on the Porch talking to his wife Martha, who is sitting with her tackety boots on, rocking on her chair and smoking her clay pipe. Both of them are surveying the land that they had fought and worked hard for and now it was all theirs.) A real happy ever after story.

Working for Nichol was a real pleasure. He taught me all about his business, from ordering from suppliers, to operating the conveyor belt that brushes and cleans the potatoes then ends in a set of automatic scales where you can set the weights to pre-pack the potatoes.

Nichol also introduced me to all his family and some-times took me on excursions with them. Lanark Market was one of the really busy and interesting places to go. Nichol bought some young pigs (weaners) on one of our visits to Lanark market.

"When did you do the bidding?" I asked him.

"That is a trade secret." He replied.

"That is also another job for you too son. Cleaning and feeding them every day. Don't worry, you will be paid more too."

"Great, when are they being delivered?" I said.

"Tomorrow." Said Nichol.

"We need to get back to the yard and prepare some pens. How many did you buy?" I ask him.

"Twelve," said Nichol.

"Good, I know what two pens we can put them in."

The next day I was at the yard at 6.30am to look at the pens I had selected. This place had been a large piggery before. Even though many of the pens had been demolished, some were still in very good repair. Round the corner from the office were two pens side by side with a water tap opposite. Perfect I thought. A lane in between the office and the pens would allow me access to the dumping area where I could barrow away any waste created by the pigs. There would be a lot of waste.

Going into the office to put the tea urn on for everyone arriving at the yard, the phone is ringing. I answer it and the caller says he is the float driver delivering the pigs and he would be there in an hour. Goodness sake, I still need to check the locks on the pen gates, also, I need to get some bedding into both pens.

Locks are all good, bedding is in both pens and fresh water is in the troughs. We are ready for the arrivals.

One hour later the pigs are happily in their new homes. Nichol is delighted with my efforts and said he would give me a bonus when the pigs get sold. Every night after school I am there feeding and cleaning out the pigs. If any tatties need to be bagged for the next day, I get involved in that too. Weekends are as normal, Barlanark on a Friday night, Carntyne on a Saturday morning, Sunday, feeding pigs and bagging tatties. My tin under Sanny's bed is getting very heavy and full now. Two weeks of Easter holidays had earned me more money than I had ever seen. I am rich beyond my wildest dreams. So I thought anyway.

Nichol is taking me with his family to The Edinburgh Highland Show at Ingliston. I cannot wait to go there.

Getting ready for Nichol to pick me up for that trip, I discovered the toes were worn out of my shoes. Mam, as ever, very resourceful, gave me the oul man's brown suede shoes to wear. I am a four in a shoe, the oul man is a six.

With two pairs of thick socks and a cutout cardboard insole, my shoes are fitting a bit better but still slapping on the pavement as I plod out to the van. Nichol's older brother Jimmy is sitting in the back of the van with me and it is not long before he clocks the shoes I have on.

"You are looking very suave the day, son." He said.

"Leave Davie alone Jimmy, you are not so smart yourself, are you? Will I tell Davie you had to borrow my shirt and jacket this morning?"

Jimmy, embarrassed himself now, turned and said to me,

"Sorry wee man." He reached out and shook my hand.

Jimmy and I got on like a house on fire after that.

The Highland Show was brilliant for me as my holidays on Donal's farm had taught me a lot about agriculture.

Nichol was amazed at my work ethic and ability to absorb knowledge. He planned great things for me.

When I leave school, Nichol said I should work for him for a year or so during which time he would teach me to drive. After passing my driving test, a van would be provided for me and two days of his runs given over to me also. This would give me an opportunity at a young age to start and build my own business in a market that I was well versed in. The only stipulation he made was that I should buy my produce from him.

Nichol's brother Jimmy had already been doing this for two years and said to me he was making an excellent income.

Just prior to leaving school I was looking for advice from my well travelled Uncle Johnny.

"Listen to me son, if you want a nice quiet life, do not employ anyone and never argue with the Police." He said.

This little gem has stood me in good stead and I have passed this message on, many times.

The oul man and a completely uninterested careers officer advised me to get an apprenticeship, as I was leaving school with no qualifications.

If they had let me explain to them the knowledge I had gained in driving, agriculture, swine husbandry, customer services, purchase ordering, stock rotation and production line management. Maybe the advice, guidance and direction I was given, would have been a lot better. The careers officer asked me if I knew what time it was.

"Yes, it's four thirty."

"You better get a move on then before all the decorators close for the night."

The week before school broke up for the summer of 1966 I was fifteen and planned to go round all the decorating businesses in Coatbridge to look for a painting and decorating job. The first place I went to was near Sunnyside cross. I was told to start the following week. No instructions, just be here at 8 oclock Monday morning with your whites on. I was hardly going to decorate the world on a weekly pay of £4 3\9. or £5 per week clear if I worked on a Sunday.

My painting career is a story for another time.

Nichol and his family were all extremely disappointed with my decision.

Over the years to come, with many different career paths in lots of different industries behind me, I would live to regret that decision a lot of times. Nichol continued his business for many more years although he never gave any of his future employees the same offer as me.

I really hope the reader has enjoyed this story. This is not the end as I have many more exploits to tell about my farm holidays and my life growing up poor but happy in a large family, in the town of Coatbridge, which was also known as.

"THE IRON BURGH."

Laborare est orare.

Epilogue

Coatbridge is a very different place now. The town has gone through many changes since 1951 when I was born. Some of my family still live in the town so my wife Martha (who is also from Coatbridge) and I, still visit frequently. We visit the Summerlee Heritage Museum quite often where I recognise many of the exhibits. A steam engine my father drove in RB Tennents foundry at Whifflet is on display there. Another one is on display at a railway museum in Boness near grangemouth.

Writing this book has been an eye opener for me. Although leaving school at fifteen with no qualifications I still thought I was good at English. After all the advice and guidance I have needed and received from Kim and Sinclair at Indie Authors I realise I still have a lot to learn even at my age.

I look forward to any comments or feedback from readers. Maybe I will be spurred on to continue with a follow up book on the exploits of wee Davie and his family.

About the Author

David Mcclure was born in Airdrie in 1951 and brought up in Coatbridge in the shadow of Gartsherrie Iron Works. Growing up as the third oldest in a family of eleven was not easy as there was usually some crisis or other going on. His Baptist upbringing stood him in good stead. A good work ethic in those days even at a young age was always well rewarded. Starting working life off as an apprentice painter and decorator David had many career changes. The hosiery industry beckoned him with the lure of more money. Machine operating in knitwear factories and spinning mills gave him a good mechanical knowledge which was to benefit him for twenty years as a production worker with a Swedish truck and bus manufacturer. Many career changes later and Living now in Ayrshire with his wife and family retirement was never an option as along with his wife he became a full time foster carer. He is already planning a follow up to this book. In between fishing and all the other family activities.

Lightning Source UK Ltd.
Milton Keynes UK
UKHW010827201021
392527UK00002B/390